365 Pocket Prayers

Tyndale House Publishers, Inc., Carol Stream, Illinois

Visit Tyndale's exciting Web site at www.tyndale.com.

TYNDALE and Tyndale's quill logo are registered trademarks of Tyndale House Publishers, Inc. *LeatherLike* is a registered trademark of Tyndale House Publishers, Inc.

365 Pocket Prayers

Designed by Jessie McGrath

Edited by Amy Mason

Scripture quotations are taken from the *Holy Bible*, New Living Translation, copyright © 1996, 2004, 2007 by Tyndale House Foundation. Used by permission of Tyndale House Publishers, Inc., Carol Stream, Illinois 60188. All rights reserved.

ISBN 978-1-4143-3776-0

Printed in China

17 16 15 14 13 12 11
12 11 10   9   8   7   6

INTRODUCTION

Prayer is simply talking with God. We can come to him anytime and approach him anywhere. And we can pray about anything. God loves our honest, heartfelt prayers, and he cares deeply for the details of our lives. As we come before him with praise or petition, we demonstrate that we trust him and long to draw near to him.

Perhaps your faith is relatively new and you're not yet comfortable praying. This book is for you. The prayers we've developed can be claimed as your own conversations with God. As you pray through each topic and day, we hope you will become more comfortable talking with God and will even begin to form your own prayers to him.

Perhaps you've been a believer for years but need a little inspiration in your prayer life. This book is for you, too. We all have times when we repeat the same prayers over and over. By including a year's worth of unique prayers that cover a broad range of topics, this book will help rejuvenate your dialogue with God.

Thank God that we don't have to be spiritually mature or "on fire" to have a meaningful prayer life! Wherever you are in your spiritual journey, God delights when you draw near to him. We hope this little book will help you do so.

You will find 365 prayers, arranged by days and topics. You can pray through each day of the year consecutively if you wish. Alternatively, look in the index for a topic that will help you pray through an urgent need or give words to something you may be experiencing. Every few days you will also find prayers called *Prayerful Moments*. These are shorter prayers for days when time is limited or for when you need a quick word with God.

As you enter into a new prayer, take it slow. Spend some time thinking about what you're saying to God, and try to personalize each prayer for your own life. Making each written prayer your own honest praise or petition will make it more meaningful.

In your conversations with God, take some time to listen. Reading God's Word as a part of your prayer time gives the Lord an opportunity to speak to you, too. You won't want to miss what he has to say! We've included a Scripture verse at the end of each prayer to help you ponder what God might be communicating to you.

Thank you for joining us on this quest for a deeper prayer life. It is our hope that by the end of this book, you will be inspired in your conversations with God and—most important—feel closer to him than ever before. It is often in these special times of prayer that God does his powerful work in our hearts. So don't give up; stick with it. As his Word says to us, "Let us come boldly to the throne of our gracious God. There we will receive his mercy, and we will find grace to help us when we need it most" (Hebrews 4:16).

The privilege of prayer is that it ushers us straight into the presence of our loving God. And Scripture promises us that he won't disappoint! With that in mind, it's time to begin.

DAY 1

☀ **A prayer for GROWTH**
When I want to grow spiritually

DEAR GOD,

I confess that I often want to be instantly mature in my faith. I lack the patience to work at it. Help me to remember that spiritual growth is like physical growth: I must start small, take one day at a time, and get enough nourishment. I know I can do this by challenging my mind to study your Word, asking questions about it, and then seeking answers through prayer, the counsel of other believers, and life's experiences. Help me to see each day as a building block and to commit to building a life of godly character one step at a time.

We ask God to give you complete knowledge of his will and to give you spiritual wisdom and understanding. Then the way you live will always honor and please the Lord, and your lives will produce every kind of good fruit. All the while, you will grow as you learn to know God better and better. COLOSSIANS 1:9-10

DAY 2

☼ **A prayer about INITIATIVE**
How does God continue to initiate a relationship with me?

HOLY GOD,

I believe that you sometimes initiate a change of heart in me so that I will desire to be in closer relationship with you. Selfish ambition and spiritual blindness steal my passion for you, and sometimes you need to point out these ways within me. Your Holy Spirit convicts me of my sin, prompting me to remember you, confess my waywardness, and seek restoration with you. Lord God, thank you that you take the initiative in this way. But you don't only point out the offense; you also guide me back to the right path. You never initiate a change of heart and then abandon me. Thank you for constantly taking the first step. No matter how many times I wander, you are always ready to take me back and restore me into a right relationship with you.

"My wayward children," says the LORD, "come back to me, and I will heal your wayward hearts." JEREMIAH 3:22

☀ **A prayer of ANTICIPATION**
When I wonder what great things God has planned for me

O GOD,

My life is so noisy—and sadly, it resounds more often with ringing phones and droning televisions than with praise and worship for you. Do I ever pause and wonder what momentous things you might be preparing to do next in my life? How many moments of awe-inspiring anticipation do I miss by never being still before you? I need your help to discipline myself. Help me to build a few moments of silent anticipation into each day, making time to pray and open myself up to what you want to do in and through me. I pray, God, that in these moments, you will reveal enough of your plan to make me ready for your great purposes in my life. I come before you with reverent awe and anticipation for the glorious future that lies ahead.

You guide me with your counsel, leading me to a glorious destiny. PSALM 73:24

DAY 4

☀ **A prayer about CHALLENGES**
When I need to see how challenges will shape me

O LORD,

Thank you for your Word. How often we see our own struggles through the lives of the people in the Bible. I'm encouraged by the example of Paul, whose goal to preach the gospel in new places continually brought him fresh challenges. While difficult, those trials clearly caused greater growth in his relationship with you. Lord, what do you want me to learn from the challenges that come my way? And how might they strengthen my relationship with you? Please show me how to step out in faith so that I can move closer to you. May the struggles I face cause me to follow your leading into uncharted waters, and may I learn to trust you more and more. Then I know I will be accomplishing your unique purpose for me. Thank you for showing me that it is often through challenges that you make your plan clear to me.

Be strong and courageous, and do the work. Don't be afraid or discouraged, for the LORD God . . . is with you. He will not fail you or forsake you. I CHRONICLES 28:20

✳ **A prayer for HOPE**
When I need to fix my eyes on the hope of eternity

ETERNAL GOD AND SAVIOR,

For a prisoner on death row, a pardon offers hope of freedom. I was once a spiritual prisoner facing eternal death because of my sin. You have given me the ultimate hope of freedom by forgiving my sins so I can one day be with you forever in heaven. How can I thank you enough? When my life here and now seems impossible, you give eternal hope. Without hope, I could not persevere through the tough times. I would give up. As I walk through this life, may I fix my eyes on eternity. May I never forget where I am headed, and why there is no better place to be. For in heaven I will live in perfect relationship with you and others forever, with no pain or sorrow or suffering. What joy! Please help me to move straight ahead toward that goal. As I do, I know I'll gain a better perspective on the struggles and discomforts of this life.

All praise to God, the Father of our Lord Jesus Christ. It is by his great mercy that we have been born again, because God raised Jesus Christ from the dead. Now we live with great expectation, and we have a priceless inheritance—an inheritance that is kept in heaven for you, pure and undefiled, beyond the reach of change and decay. And through your faith, God is protecting you by his power until you receive this salvation. . . . There is wonderful joy ahead, even though you have to endure many trials for a little while. 1 PETER 1:3-6

☼ **A prayer of CONFESSION**
 When I have a guilty conscience

MERCIFUL GOD,

I'm feeling guilty and my conscience is showing me that it's time to confess my wrongdoing. I know you are prompting me to seek forgiveness. I'm sorry for the wrong I've done. I am so grateful that you don't shut me out when I have sinned. Even my sin can be an opportunity for you to pursue me and call me back to your righteous path. Thank you, God, for removing my guilt, restoring my joy, and healing my broken soul.

People who conceal their sins will not prosper, but if they confess and turn from them, they will receive mercy.
PROVERBS 28:13

DAY 7 *Prayerful Moment*

☼ **A prayer about GOALS**
 How can goals help me move forward spiritually?

DEAR GOD,

Often I set long-term and short-term goals, but can I also set eternal goals? Shouldn't I spend more time thinking about my future home with you? Father, show me how to set goals that will keep me moving forward spiritually!

All athletes are disciplined in their training. They do it to win a prize that will fade away, but we do it for an eternal prize. I CORINTHIANS 9:25

☀ **A prayer about the CALL OF GOD**
When I wonder if God has a calling for me

DEAR GOD,

Deep down inside, I long to be a part of something bigger than myself. I sometimes wonder why I was born and what I should be doing with my life. I believe my search for purpose is actually the result of you calling me to discover the reason you created me. I often wish, God, that your call would come in the form of an audible voice or a miraculous sign in the sky. But that's not usually the way you communicate, and you don't always call people to extraordinary, life-changing adventures. Your call is often a task right in front of me, something I can do today; it might be working in the nursery at church, caring for an ailing parent, giving kind instructions to a child, making dinner at a local soup kitchen, or volunteering at a my child's school. Lord, you have given me special gifts and abilities, and you want me to use them now, not just five or ten years from now. Help me to answer your call to serve you and other people today so that I might be fully prepared when you call me to something bigger. Thank you that in everything you call me to do, you will equip me with the desire, vision, support, and resources I need to carry it out.

May the God of peace make you holy in every way, and may your whole spirit and soul and body be kept blameless until our Lord Jesus Christ comes again. God will make this happen, for he who calls you is faithful.
I THESSALONIANS 5:23-24

☀ A prayer about ABILITIES
When I want to maximize my God-given abilities

LORD,

I may not be the strongest, the fastest, the smartest, or the most beautiful, but I know you can still use me in a powerful way. Teach me that the abilities you have given me are only maximized when they are used for your purposes. Please reveal to me my abilities and my spiritual gifts. I want to learn how to use those gifts for you, not just for myself, so I can realize what it means to honor and serve you. Show me how to fit my abilities into your plan, so that my life will yield great results in your eyes.

When someone has been given much, much will be required in return; and when someone has been entrusted with much, even more will be required. LUKE 12:48

☀ **A prayer about TITHING**
When I set aside my gifts for God

DEAR GOD,

Each year as I determine how I can give to you financially, I consider what I receive from giving. I know that supporting the church and the work of godly people around the world can provide great joy. Also, I want to give to you because you truly are my number one priority, and I am so grateful for the blessings you have given me. I know that maintaining a habit of regular tithing will help remind me that you are the source of all my blessings. God, as I commit my tithes to you, I ask that you use my gifts to support your work in my community and around the world to meet the needs of those less fortunate than I am. By my gifts, may I show my commitment to you and honor you for your faithful provision in my life.

Give, and you will receive. Your gift will return to you in full—pressed down, shaken together to make room for more, running over, and poured into your lap. The amount you give will determine the amount you get back. LUKE 6:38

DAY 11

☼ A prayer about ACCOMPLISHMENTS
When I want to accomplish what will truly last

DEAR LORD,

Deep within my heart lies a longing for real significance and purpose—a longing that you have given me. But too often I have much lower ambitions. Why is my first instinct to look out for myself? Why does that come so easily? It's more difficult, more costly, but more significant to look out for others. I know that, but I need your help to do it. Whenever I think about myself first, I waste an opportunity to have eternal impact. Please grant me the awareness to know if my actions are accomplishing what glorifies myself—and will therefore never last beyond this life—or what glorifies you and will stand for all eternity. Lord, please give me a heart that seeks your glory.

[Those who are rich] should be rich in good works and generous to those in need, always being ready to share with others. By doing this they will be storing up their treasure as a good foundation for the future so that they may experience true life. 1 TIMOTHY 6:18-19

DAY 12

☀ **A prayer for TRANSFORMATION**
When I don't know what to do with my worst enemy

LORD,

The person who has hurt me the most keeps coming to mind. My guess is that you have something to do with that. And I don't think you are bringing him to mind so I can plan how to hurt him, but rather so I can pray for him. Is it possible you could change this person into a loving, on-fire believer? I don't doubt that you can. If you can turn the murderer Saul into the apostle Paul, you can certainly do a work of transformation in my greatest enemy. You are the God of transformation! But too often, in my sinful nature, I don't want you to do your work of healing and change in others. Help me to be eager for transformed lives. Lord, the next time I find myself hating that person who makes my life miserable, transform my heart so that I pray for him instead. Then don't let me be surprised if I see you begin to change him. I know you'll be changing me, too!

The Lord said, "Go over to Straight Street, to the house of Judas. When you get there, ask for a man from Tarsus named Saul. . . . I have shown him a vision of a man named Ananias coming in and laying hands on him so he can see again." "But Lord," exclaimed Ananias, "I've heard many people talk about the terrible things this man has done to the believers in Jerusalem! . . ." But the Lord said, "Go, for Saul is my chosen instrument to take my message to the Gentiles and to kings, as well as to the people of Israel."
ACTS 9:11-15

☼ A prayer for the PRESENCE OF GOD
When I want to experience more of God's presence in my life

LORD,

You are the great and awesome Creator of all. Yet you invite me to call on you without hesitation. You say that if I am sincere in wanting to know you—rather than just looking for a good-luck charm or magic genie—you will reveal yourself to me. This is why you are the only one I will worship and adore.

The LORD is close to all who call on him, yes, to all who call on him in truth. PSALM 145:18

DAY 14 *Prayerful Moment*

☼ A prayer about MEDITATION
When I want to remain focused in my spiritual walk

LORD,

Teach me the discipline of meditating on you and on your Word. How can I be spiritually focused if I can't control my thoughts? And how can I ever hope to understand your will for me if I don't listen to what you say? Help me to push my own thoughts and desires aside and allow your Spirit to speak to me. Guide my heart and remind me of your presence. May my thoughts always be fixed on you!

You will keep in perfect peace all who trust in you, all whose thoughts are fixed on you! ISAIAH 26:3

DAY 15

☼ **A prayer for VISION**
*When I need a clearer vision of what God wants
me to be*

DEAR GOD,

I want to have purpose. I want to see my way clearly in life; I want to be motivated to do something that counts. O Lord, I need vision—a picture of where you want me to be at some point in the future. How do I more clearly see what you created me to accomplish? It's only when I empty myself of my own dreams that you can fill me with your vision of my future. Please help me. May I empty myself by keeping your Word before me each day, by having a clear conscience so I can more clearly hear the promptings of your Spirit, by listening to the godly wisdom of other believers, and by praying—communing directly with you. Oh, grant me the ability to believe that you have a purpose for me to achieve and a definite place where you want my life to go. Is there any vision more meaningful than that?

Open my eyes to see. PSALM 119:18

⚙ **A prayer about WORK**
When I need to discover more meaning in my work

O GOD,

When I'm bored, I feel so unproductive. Even though my work seems overwhelming sometimes, I thank you for it. I know it is part of your plan for my life, and I know that it matters to you. When I work diligently, I experience meaning and joy that I'm able to pass on to others. May I always remember that my work should model characteristics of *your* work, such as excellence, concern for the well-being of others, purpose, beauty, and service. Help me to remember that I am actually working for you. Then I can focus less on the task itself and more on what my real motives should be—to help people know you. The excitement and interest that come from having this perspective are not primarily from my work itself but from the one for whom I work. So as I do my work, may I be a credible witness to those around me. May I see my work as an opportunity to serve you and others.

Work willingly at whatever you do, as though you were working for the Lord rather than for people. Remember that the Lord will give you an inheritance as your reward, and that the Master you are serving is Christ.
COLOSSIANS 3:23-24

DAY 17

⚙ **A prayer for BEGINNINGS**
When I seek a fresh start

LORD GOD,

At some point, all people dream of new beginnings—an escape from sameness, a chance to wipe the slate clean and start over, an opportunity to move away from past hurts, or maybe just a chance to do something different. Sometimes a new beginning is threatening because it forces me away from what is known and comfortable. Other times it is exciting—a challenge to move into new territory, or the exhilaration of an unknown adventure. Lord, you're showing me that life is really a series of new beginnings. Please remind me that change is inevitable; it's how I deal with it that counts. Each day brings new challenges and problems. Each day also brings new opportunities to get to know you better, God, and to start over with a new attitude toward my circumstances and the people around me. Lord, because you renew your mercies to me every single day, I don't have to be burdened by yesterday's failures or regrets. Help me to embrace the dawn of each new day as a chance to start again and to experience the refreshment of your tender mercies.

Great is his faithfulness; his mercies begin afresh each morning. LAMENTATIONS 3:23

☼ A prayer about QUIET TIMES
When God doesn't seem to be showing up for quiet times

LORD,

I admit that I struggle to be still and quiet. I want to hear you speak, but I know that so often I throw out my complaints or needs and then rush on with my day without even listening for your response. Help me to prepare myself to hear you speak. Honestly, I feel awkward just sitting there and not talking. Please empty me of my need to be heard or to be in control of our times together. May I just spend time in your presence without verbalizing my prayers. Teach me to meditate on you and listen for your voice. Help me to believe that I will hear you, and ready my heart to hear you speak to me.

I wait quietly before God, for my victory comes from him. . . . Let all that I am wait quietly before God, for my hope is in him. . . . Pour out your heart to him, for God is our refuge.
PSALM 62:1, 5, 8

☀ **A prayer in times of SPIRITUAL DRYNESS**
When I thirst for God

O LORD,
My soul is thirsty. I feel so dry, longing for something that will be truly fulfilling. My desire to know you and serve you has wilted and dried up. As a farmer takes extra care of his fields in a drought, so I am in desperate need of some extra soul care during this time of spiritual dryness. The best place to go for that is your Word. As I read it, may it water my soul, soaking in and filling me with divine nourishment. May it speak to me and renew my sense of purpose. I pray that you would also send opportunities for service to revive my passion for you. When you do, push me off the sidelines and into the work you want me to do. Don't let me miss out. That is what I need to get serious about my faith again. O Lord, my parched soul longs for you. Let me drink deeply now.

The LORD will guide you continually, giving you water when you are dry and restoring your strength. You will be like a well-watered garden, like an ever-flowing spring. ISAIAH 58:11

☀ **A prayer about ABSOLUTE TRUTH**
When I don't know what is true

HEAVENLY FATHER,

History is full of examples of individuals who did what was right in their own eyes—with catastrophic results! I know that I am born with the desire to sin, and that doing my own thing will always lead me away from you, the source of all truth. Teach me not to pass judgment on your ways by devising my own, but to follow you in every way. Help me to follow your instructions, for your truth will last forever.

All he does is just and good, and all his commandments are trustworthy. They are forever true, to be obeyed faithfully and with integrity. PSALM 111:7-8

DAY 21 *Prayerful Moment*

☀ **A prayer for PATIENCE**
When patience doesn't come naturally

LORD,

I need patience! I am so focused on my own agenda and priorities, and I get impatient when life doesn't go the way I want it to. Remind me that there is more to life than maintaining a schedule. Open my eyes to your perspective, Lord, so I can have peace, no matter the circumstances.

We also pray that you will be strengthened with all his glorious power so you will have all the endurance and patience you need. COLOSSIANS 1:11

⚙ **A prayer about POTENTIAL**
   When I want to see the potential God sees in me

DEAR GOD,

Reading the book of Judges I am struck at how your angel greeted Gideon by calling him "mighty hero." Was he talking to the right person? Gideon was hiding from his enemies, the Midianites, and he saw himself as the least important in his family. But when you looked at Gideon, you saw the man who would rescue Israel. Lord, do you look at me that way? Am I a "mighty hero" in your eyes even though I think of myself as weak? Oh, please bring out the best in me! Thank you that you see more in me than I see in myself. I look at my limitations, but you, O God, look at my potential. You perceive in me what you created me to be. Thank you for seeing what I can become instead of scolding me for who I am. It makes me want to rise to your expectations and become a person who models a giant faith. May I aspire to reflect all you see in me.

The angel of the LORD came. . . . Gideon son of Joash was threshing wheat at the bottom of a winepress to hide the grain from the Midianites. The angel of the LORD appeared to him and said, "Mighty hero, the LORD is with you!"
JUDGES 6:11-12

☼ **A prayer for MERCY**
When I need to grasp the mercy of God

LORD,

I am such a sinner. If I'm honest with myself, I admit that sin affects everything I do. It penetrates most of my thoughts. When you see how sin has infected me—and everyone on earth—it must break your heart. We are all so prone to ignore you, neglect you, even rebel against you. Why would you want to risk all this rejection? It can only be because of your infinite love and mercy. Out of your love comes the mercy that gives me a second chance even when I don't deserve it. And it's not just a *second* chance. Again and again you reach out to me in love, no matter how many times my sin drives a wedge between us. Even though my sin and rebellion against you deserve punishment, you offer forgiveness and eternal life instead. The more I understand that you show mercy even when I don't deserve it, the more I will experience the full impact of your love for me. Only then will I be able to truly love others and show them mercy, even when they don't deserve it.

The LORD is compassionate and merciful, slow to get angry and filled with unfailing love. He will not constantly accuse us, nor remain angry forever. He does not punish us for all our sins; he does not deal harshly with us, as we deserve. PSALM 103:8-10

DAY 24

☼ A prayer about HABITS
When I want to develop a habit of reading my Bible

DEAR FATHER,

Just as I am in the habit of eating every day, help me develop the habit of feeding on your Word every day. Your Scriptures nourish my soul and quench my spiritual thirst. You promise that your Word is living, penetrating every fiber of my being. It provides the antidote for the deadly disease of sin; it shows me how to thrive with joy; it develops in me a clean and holy heart. Without the habit of reading my Bible, I know I will inevitably drift away from you. Please don't let this happen, for if I am apart from you, I will have no chance to experience the mercy and blessings that come from a relationship with you. Grant me this prayer, Lord—not just a habit of reading your Word, but a deep desire to be drawn to it every day.

All Scripture is inspired by God and is useful to teach us what is true and to make us realize what is wrong in our lives. It corrects us when we are wrong and teaches us to do what is right. God uses it to prepare and equip his people to do every good work. 2 TIMOTHY 3:16-17

DAY 25

☀ **A prayer of TRUST**
When I need to trust God more

DEAR LORD,

There are so few people I really trust. And if I'm honest, I have to ask if I fully trust you, especially when tough times come into my life. Distrust is so painful because it causes me to question others' motives. But trust is a beautiful gift. When I trust others, our relationships are deepened because I know that what they tell me is true and that they are acting in my best interest. If I can't trust you, O God, the only one who is completely trustworthy, I will never experience true peace, and I won't be able to engage in a relationship with you. Help me to trust you, for you alone are trustworthy. When I learn to trust you, I will never have to question your motives. Lord, may I be absolutely confident that you always have my best interests in mind because your love for me is so great.

Those who know your name trust in you, for you, O LORD, do not abandon those who search for you. PSALM 9:10

DAY 26

⚙ **A prayer of BELONGING**
My loving obedience is proof I belong to God

DEAR GOD,

I know that obeying you is an important part of belonging to you, because it shows others that I love you. It is out of love that you give commands to your people, to protect us, guide us, and ensure that we experience life to the fullest. Obeying you is a sign that I have accepted your call and that I belong to you. Disobeying you is not so much about breaking a law as breaking your heart by showing that I love myself more than you. God, you are my heavenly Father, who welcomes me into your family and showers me with blessings as I obey you. These blessings may not always be material things, but they are always rich and satisfying—such as peace of mind, lasting joy, and the honor of experiencing your presence. I'm so grateful to belong to you, and I want to show it. Thank you for sharing the blessings that come from belonging to your family.

Keep the way of the LORD by doing what is right and just. Then I will do . . . all that I have promised.
GENESIS 18:19

☼ **A prayer about the HOLY SPIRIT**
  When I need divine wisdom

DEAR JESUS,

Thank you for sending the Holy Spirit to be my spiritual mentor and guide. Through your Spirit, you help me build my relationship with you and guide me into wisdom, understanding, and spiritual maturity. I invite your Spirit to lead me so that I can grow in faith and wisdom.

You have received the Holy Spirit, and he lives within you, so you don't need anyone to teach you what is true. For the Spirit teaches you everything you need to know, and what he teaches is true—it is not a lie. So just as he has taught you, remain in fellowship with Christ. 1 JOHN 2:27

DAY 28 *Prayerful Moment*

☼ **A prayer in TEMPTATION**
  When I feel under spiritual attack

LORD,

One of Satan's favorite strategies is to make sin look desirable, harmless, and good. He knows exactly how to entice me, and he takes advantage of every weakness. Don't let Satan trick me with his lies! Help me to stay strong through the work of your Spirit. As I seek your guidance, show me that the enemy is no match for your power within me.

Keep watch and pray, so that you will not give in to temptation. For the spirit is willing, but the body is weak! MATTHEW 26:41

DAY 29

☼ **A prayer about SIN**
  When I struggle with the concept of being sinful

GOD,

Why do I sometimes feel like *sin* is such an offensive word? I can talk about crimes like theft or murder; I can calculate statistics about adultery, unwed mothers, and divorce; I can trivialize greed, selfishness, and lust—but to call anything *sin* makes me uncomfortable. It implies the violation of an objective, absolute standard of behavior, and if I'm honest, I feel like that kind of standard is an infringement on my rights. I know my reaction displays a terrible misunderstanding of sin and an underestimation of you, God. If a doctor were to correctly diagnose a fatal disease in my body, I would not accuse him of intruding on my freedom; rather, I would be grateful because he could treat me. The Bible teaches that sin is a disease of the soul that will destroy my life if I do not treat it. God, your standards of behavior are like preventive medicine for my soul; your commandments are not meant to limit my freedom but to curtail the disease of sin. When I understand sin in this way, Lord, I am thankful that you care so deeply for my soul.

If we confess our sins to him, he is faithful and just to forgive us our sins and to cleanse us from all wickedness.

I JOHN 1:9

⚙ **A prayer about WORTH**
  When I wonder if I'm worthy enough to follow God

GOD,

I often struggle to see myself as you might. I either fail to see my faults, or I fail to see my value. I know you love me for who I am, because you created me this way! I know your love for me is not based on what I do for you, because you loved me before I made my first mistake, before I uttered my first word, and even before I took my first breath. Your love for me is an eternal thread woven throughout my life and fortified through the life, death, and resurrection of Jesus on my behalf. I still struggle with believing that your approval doesn't depend on what I do. I confess that sometimes I get so caught up in doing things for you, God, that I lose sight of the greatest privilege of all—knowing you and being known by you. To have my name registered as a citizen of heaven means that I belong, without question, to your eternal Kingdom. Nothing else I do on earth can compare with that joy. Lord, please keep me from the trap of basing my self-worth on my performance. Teach me to rejoice that it is based on your unconditional love for me.

You made [people] only a little lower than God and crowned them with glory and honor. PSALM 8:5

☼ A prayer about RELATIONSHIP
When I want to feel closer to God

DEAR GOD,

The image of love between a husband and wife or parent and child is a glimpse of the kind of relationship you want to have with me. How amazing that part of your design in relationships was to help people know how to relate to you. I want my bond with you to be stronger than with anyone else, but I struggle to know how to talk with you or feel closer to you. That's because too often I see you as a distant God. But when I think of relating to you as I do my close friends or family, I see you have given me living examples! It is through closeness with others that I learn how to be intimate, how to share my heart, thoughts, and dreams with someone else. But God, you already know those things. You know the best and the worst in me, and you saved me anyway. That alone proves you are not a distant God but a personal God who loves and pursues me. Thank you for always reaching out to me, always seeking to be close to me. Let the response of my heart be to pursue you, just as I would in any other relationship. I pray that as I do, I would begin to know you intimately. May I experience a loving relationship that is second to no other.

Moses said to the LORD, ". . . If it is true that you look favorably on me, let me know your ways so I may understand you more fully and continue to enjoy your favor."
EXODUS 33:12-13

DAY 32

⚙ **A prayer about REGRETS**
When I need to get over my regrets

O LORD,

Regret is one of the heaviest burdens I carry. I have made bad decisions that I wish I could do over. I ask you to release me from the guilt I feel about my past sins and mistakes. Free me from my chains of remorse, for you are the God of transformation and renewal. I am taking you up on your promise to help me deal with my regrets so I can move on without carrying that heavy load. Since I am a follower of Jesus, you forgive my confessed sins—all of them. And more than that, you actually forget them and give me a fresh start. Oh, how I want that. How I need that! I know the consequences of my past actions are not retractable. I can live with that if I know that I am fully forgiven and that you consider me worthy to serve you. If you don't hold my past against me, neither should I. My mind is free to look ahead and not back. I am no longer a slave to my regrets because I have thrown them off in order to do something better, more worthy, for you. After all, if Peter had been burdened by his regret after denying Jesus, he would never have been able to preach the Good News so powerfully. Thank you that you can relieve my burden too.

Oh, what joy for those whose disobedience is forgiven, whose sins are put out of sight. Yes, what joy for those whose record the LORD has cleared of sin. ROMANS 4:7-8

⚙ **A prayer about GOD'S HAND**
   *When I question if God has a hand in a particular
   situation*

O GOD,

Sometimes you have demonstrated your power through visible, miraculous signs. At other times it has been much more subtle, moving in my heart as I seek you. Sometimes you have worked through events in my life or used surprising people to accomplish your will. Sometimes you have been a still, quiet voice in my mind, and at other times you have been a force to be reckoned with. Some things about you are constant and unchanging: your love, your law, your promises. Other things about you are wild and mysterious. You have rarely worked the same way twice in my life, so I know I must trust you diligently and live with a sense of expectancy, knowing that you want to work your will through me. Often, it isn't until I look back that I can see your fingerprints. You have proved that I can trust you, and I am thankful that your hand is on me even now.

The LORD says, "I will guide you along the best pathway for your life. I will advise you and watch over you."
PSALM 32:8

☼ A prayer of AVAILABILITY
When I want to be available for God's purposes

DEAR JESUS,

To be available to you means more than just acknowledging your existence. It means reorienting my life so that no matter what I do, I do it as service to you. Jesus, please give me an eagerness to go where you call me and serve where you show me. Make my hesitant heart a willing heart. May I experience your blessings—not because of my ability, but because of my availability to you.

My sheep listen to my voice; I know them, and they follow me.
JOHN 10:27

DAY 35 *Prayerful Moment*

☼ A prayer about the PROMISES OF GOD
How does knowing God help me believe his promises?

DEAR GOD,

I often find it hard to trust in others' promises. Few people are truthful and dependable, and even if they are, sometimes life just happens and they are unable to carry out what they promised. But if I can't believe a promise from you, I can't believe a promise from anyone, because you alone are completely trustworthy. You are truth, and you have the power to carry out all you have said. Even when circumstances might lead me to doubt, please strengthen my confidence that your promises will come true.

God can be trusted to keep his promise. HEBREWS 10:23

DAY 36

☼ A prayer about EXPERIENCE
When I feel inexperienced in serving God

HEAVENLY FATHER,

Thank you that you waste nothing but use everything to further your good purposes. David's first job was shepherding—hardly the recommended grooming for a future king. Yet the lessons David learned on the hills with the sheep served him well on the throne; he ruled not as a tyrant but as a shepherd. Thank you, God, that you can use me, too, in whatever situation I find myself, and you will use my current circumstances to prepare me for future service. Even if I don't think my job, activities, or circumstances are significant now, help me remember that you may be preparing me for service later. God, I need your help to make the most of where you have put me right now. Let my service to you in the present become a time of preparation for the future you have planned for me.

I am certain that God, who began the good work within you, will continue his work until it is finally finished on the day when Christ Jesus returns. PHILIPPIANS 1:6

⚙ **A prayer about GOSSIP**
When I am convicted about gossiping

DEAR JESUS,

I have been burned by the rumors of gossip, and now I'm feeling convicted about the way I talk about others. I confess I have found it entertaining to let others in on my little secrets. But now I see that my words are meant to damage someone's reputation or make myself feel better. Sometimes I share information without even knowing if it's true! I am so sorry for the way I have fanned the flames of gossip within my own circle. I see how much hurt it causes. Forgive me, God. You are the only one who can judge a person, and I should leave that in your hands. Who am I to destroy a person's reputation based on rumor? Who am I to allow gossip to continue just so I feel like I'm in the loop? When I am tempted to gossip, remind me how much it hurt to know that others believed the rumors about me. Remind me how betrayed I felt to learn how others talked about me. Let the gossip stop with me. Give me the courage to change the subject or spin the conversation by saying something positive. I don't want to add fuel to the fire any longer. Please, Lord, let my kind words allow your grace to break through to those around me.

The Scriptures say, "If you want to enjoy life and see many happy days, keep your tongue from speaking evil and your lips from telling lies." I PETER 3:10

☼ A prayer about WORDS
When I want to control my tongue

DEAR JESUS,

I've never really considered the impact of my words. But the things I say and even the meaning behind them have enormous impact on those who hear. In a sense, my words are gifts that I can give. My words can be a gift of praise to you or a gift of encouragement to a friend. I know that I have often spoken words that are annoying, complaining, insulting, demeaning, or simply useless. I'm sorry I have been so irresponsible with my tongue. I want to make my words count. Help me to be thoughtful in my prayers to you and in my speech to others. Perhaps the greatest gift I can ever give others is not in a box covered with paper and bows but in the words I use to encourage, inspire, comfort, or challenge them.

Let everything you say be good and helpful, so that your words will be an encouragement to those who hear them.
EPHESIANS 4:29

DAY 39

☼ A prayer about APATHY
When I have lost my excitement for Jesus

LORD GOD,

My faith is lukewarm right now, and my sense of passion and purpose is gone. This apathy is like a parasite that feeds on my motivation and devours the talents and gifts you have given me. Lord, I know one of Satan's greatest lies is that following you is nothing to be excited about. That couldn't be further from the truth. It is only through serving you that my life will have meaning, energy, and purpose. Your Spirit is a driving force within me, lighting a passion for service in my heart and encouraging purpose rather than boredom. God, your Word describes the antidote to apathy: purposeful work, a thankful heart, and service to others. These three things can help me fight off feelings of apathy, renew my focus on your purpose for my life, and anticipate with excitement the blessings you have in store for me. Please revive me, Lord!

God is not unjust. He will not forget how hard you have worked for him and how you have shown your love to him by caring for other believers, as you still do. Our great desire is that you will keep on loving others as long as life lasts, in order to make certain that what you hope for will come true. Then you will not become spiritually dull and indifferent.
HEBREWS 6:10-12

DAY 40

☼ **A prayer about REPUTATION**
When my reputation is at stake

DEAR GOD,

Sometimes I think that what I do in my personal life does not matter as long as I perform well on the job or look good in public. But you do not make a distinction between the way we should act in public or in private. I know that I will develop a good reputation when I display the same godly integrity alone as I do in front of others. What matters most is not what other people think of me but what you think of me. I want to develop the strong character you want me to have, with characteristics that reflect you—like justice, righteousness, integrity, mercy, honesty, fairness, and faithfulness. Lord, please give me the character to be a person of integrity at all times, not just when others are watching. Only then will I understand what it means to walk with you.

Work willingly at whatever you do, as though you were working for the Lord rather than for people. Remember that the Lord will give you an inheritance as your reward, and that the Master you are serving is Christ.
COLOSSIANS 3:23-24

⚜ **A prayer of COMMITMENT**
   Why can't I stay committed to Christ?

HEAVENLY FATHER,

Help me to get it through my head that commitment involves giving you my whole self—body, soul, emotions, and mind. Though my mind must decide to commit to you, it's my will that allows me to follow through. I know commitment can be costly, but you promise great blessings to those who are faithful. I want to be fully devoted to you—no matter what. This is my fervent prayer today.

Give yourselves completely to God, for you were dead, but now you have new life. So use your whole body as an instrument to do what is right for the glory of God.
ROMANS 6:13

DAY 42 *Prayerful Moment*

⚜ **A prayer about PERFECTION**
   When I don't feel perfect enough to serve God

DEAR GOD,

I can be such a perfectionist! Why do I feel the need to control everyone and everything? I know you love to work through imperfect people and circumstances, and that the biggest disasters are often your best opportunities. When I think about it that way, Lord, it's a relief to know that you have everything under control. Help me to trust you.

Even perfection has its limits, but your commands have no limit. PSALM 119:96

DAY 43

☀ **A prayer about VALUES**
   When I'm considering what is important in life

LORD,

Do I value the things that you consider important, useful, and worthy? Sometimes I let the world around me tell me what is important and worth pursuing. It's so easy to go with the cultural flow and even become a fearful slave to the ways of the world. How can I be so blind to the motivations within my own heart? My values are crystal clear to those around me. What I do, where I spend my time and money, and what I talk about shows exactly what I value the most. Lord, I choose to value you most. Let that decision be reflected in the words I speak and in how I spend my time, energy, and money. Help me to value what you consider to be most important: loving and worshiping you, obeying you wholeheartedly, making godly choices, and serving others.

Wherever your treasure is, there the desires of your heart will also be. LUKE 12:34

☼ **A prayer about TIME**
When I need to spend my time more wisely

O GOD,

Time is so valuable, yet I often live as though I have more than enough. I admit I waste far too much time doing things that aren't important. I let interruptions rule the day. I know I should be more purposeful about how I spend my time, but I'm often unsure how to do that. Help me to remember that you do not ask me to do everything—just everything you have called me to do. And you assure me that there is enough time for that. The more time I invest in discovering the purpose for which you created me and in living out that purpose with obedience and responsibility, the more meaningful and significant my time on earth will be. O Lord, I commit to having you as my number one priority. I want to invest in you with the best of my time and energy.

Teach us to realize the brevity of life, so that we may grow in wisdom. PSALM 90:12

☼ A prayer about the SOVEREIGNTY OF GOD
When I wonder if God is really in control

GOD,

There is a deep wound in my past, and for a long time I have held you responsible. I couldn't understand why I had to go through that experience, so I refused to trust you fully. I have blamed you for bringing that hurt into my life. I'm sorry, Lord. I see now that the pain I experienced was the result of my sinful choices, and that I was the one who was out of control, not you. Nothing I ever do can put me outside the realm of your sovereign rule. Even more amazing is your readiness to forgive me. God, please forgive my lack of self-control and my lack of faith. I am ready to turn over that hurt to you and trust your supreme control over all parts of my life. Thank you for helping me let go of the weight of my past. Thank you for the freedom that comes from trusting your sovereign rule over every moment of my life.

Trust in the LORD with all your heart; do not depend on your own understanding. Seek his will in all you do, and he will show you which path to take. PROVERBS 3:5-6

DAY 46

☼ **A prayer about DESIRABILITY**
When I want someone to love me

O LOVING GOD,

How I long to feel wanted. Desired. Pursued. Oh, but you remind me that I am. For your Word tells me that my very existence is proof of your passionate, faithful love for me. You created me in your own image to have a relationship with you. You wanted me. When I was dead in sin, you gave your Son to die for me, and you raised him to life to bring me back to you. And not only that, you have given me the Holy Spirit to satisfy my longing soul. Thank you, God! You equipped me with certain abilities to use for your special purposes. When I ignore how you made me, I miss out on the very characteristics that make me a desirable person. O Lord, thank you that you care deeply for me. All that is desirable about me comes from you.

He loves us with unfailing love; the LORD's faithfulness endures forever. Praise the LORD! PSALM 117:2

DAY 47

☼ A prayer for AFFIRMATION
When I need love and attention

DEAR GOD IN HEAVEN,

Please show me that you are also here on earth with me. I could use a little affirmation right now. No one seems to be paying much attention to me, and it feels like my hard work goes unnoticed. I want to know that my life is valued by others. But maybe there is a divine reason for this aloneness I feel. Could it be that you are reminding me that you are the best source of affirmation? You, the almighty God, chose to create me in your image and long to be in relationship with me. You sent your own Son to die for my sins so that I could have the opportunity to live with you forever. That's love and attention! Thank you that your words in the Bible and your actions toward me affirm that you desire my very heart and soul. I'm so grateful that I matter to you. Help me to notice all the little ways you break into my day with a blessing here and an encouragement there. As I learn to see with *spiritual eyes* the daily evidence of your love for me, the more confident and affirmed I will feel. I thank you and praise you that you truly care for me.

Surely your goodness and unfailing love will pursue me all the days of my life. PSALM 23:6

❄ **A prayer of LOVE**
When I want to grow in my love for others

DEAR LORD,

I confess that my first instinct is to take care of myself. Is that why you told us to love our neighbors as ourselves? Help me to fulfill your commandment by seeking to meet the needs of others the same way I seek to meet my own. I know that caring for others is what loving my neighbor is all about. Help me to see that when I show love to others, you are able to touch several hearts—theirs and mine.

It is good when you obey the royal law as found in the Scriptures: "Love your neighbor as yourself." JAMES 2:8

DAY 49 *Prayerful Moment*

❄ **A prayer about ROMANCE**
Where is the passion in a faith relationship with God?

DEAR GOD,

It is a wonderful feeling when another person expresses affection for me. When I know that someone truly enjoys my company and is captivated by me, I feel confident and secure, and I long to return the affection. As I read the Bible, I am amazed to see that you, too, are a romantic who desires intimate relationships. Father, as I realize my value to you, ignite in my heart a deep hunger to know you.

The LORD said to Israel: "I have loved you, my people, with an everlasting love. With unfailing love I have drawn you to myself." JEREMIAH 31:3

DAY 50

☼ A prayer about HARD-HEARTEDNESS
When I worry that my heart is becoming hard and stubborn

DEAR LORD,

Please don't let my heart become hard. Please show me how to evaluate the condition of my heart constantly so it remains a place where you want to reside. Is my heart becoming more hard and stubborn or more compassionate and merciful? Would others say, "There goes someone with the heart of Jesus"? I want a heart that is open to your counsel, that humbly accepts criticism, and that boldly rejects the tempting offers to sin. May I not find it difficult to forgive others. May I not find it difficult to see you at work in my daily life. When these things happen, then I fear my heart may be hardening. And that is my greatest fear, for a hard heart cuts me off from receiving your grace and forgiveness. A hard heart rejects your love, which is the only thing that can save it. Please, O Lord, keep my heart right with you.

I will give you a new heart, and I will put a new spirit in you. I will take out your stony, stubborn heart and give you a tender, responsive heart. EZEKIEL 36:26

☀ **A prayer for DEPENDENCE**
When I want to depend more on God

O LORD,

May I daily live with a constant sense of your presence. May my life be a moment-by-moment conversation with you, even as I go about my work. Teach me to pray throughout the day, offering up thanks, praise, thoughts, and requests. Help me to pause regularly to consider how you have been with me the past hour, as that will remind me to ask for your guidance in the hour ahead. Hour by hour, day by day, I want to grow more dependent upon you, O God, because your very breath sustains me. You created me for a purpose, and I want to stay close enough to you to know it and fulfill it. In my dependence on you, let me experience the freedom of life as you meant it to be.

Blessed are those who trust in the LORD and have made the LORD their hope and confidence. They are like trees planted along a riverbank, with roots that reach deep into the water. Such trees are not bothered by the heat or worried by long months of drought. Their leaves stay green, and they never stop producing fruit. JEREMIAH 17:7-8

DAY 52

☼ **A prayer about RISK**
When I need to risk more in my relationship with God

DEAR LORD,

I must admit that I don't like a lot of risk. I try to minimize it, because trying something new is scary for me if I don't know the outcome. But I know that without taking risks, nothing significant is ever accomplished. After all, the Bible says that the Christian life itself is risky; it involves trusting in a God I can't see, or taking a stand for what is right. Lord, where do I need to take more risks with you? I don't want to miss an opportunity you have for me because I was too cautious to step out in faith and follow your call. May the risks I take have a worthy goal. When you call me to do something that is out of my comfort zone, help me to obey you despite the risk of failing, and then trust you to help me succeed. The moment of risk will be worth the growth in my relationship with you.

Commit everything you do to the LORD. Trust him, and he will help you. PSALM 37:5

☼ A prayer about ADVERSITY
When I need to face the troubles that will come my way

O GOD,

Please don't let the trials of life defeat me. Instead, let them make me stronger. Please help me see adversity with the proper perspective. It comes in a multitude of ways—accidents, sickness, calamities, disappointments, failures, grief, hard times, hurts, misfortunes. But this shouldn't surprise me. You tell me in your Word that adversity *will* come, for a variety of reasons. Sometimes you send trials as a consequence for sin or as a way to strengthen my character. Other times Satan may send adversity to try to get me to sin, and sometimes I bring trouble on myself by acting foolishly or sinfully. Others' poor decisions or sin can bring adversity as well. I guess the one thing I can count on is that adversity will come! O Lord, may I understand that avoiding difficult times may not always be best for me. Though trials don't feel good, if I don't let them defeat me, they will in fact make me stronger. And may I always remember that you not only care for me during times of adversity, but you have promised to be with me through them.

When you go through deep waters, I will be with you.
When you go through rivers of difficulty, you will not drown.
When you walk through the fire of oppression, you will not be burned up; the flames will not consume you.
ISAIAH 43:2

⚙ **A prayer about DEPRESSION**
Where is God in my darkness?

MERCIFUL GOD,

I know depression because I've been there. It can descend slowly and hang in the air like an all-day rain. It can overwhelm like an avalanche of darkness. It can be the result of a specific experience of failure or loss, or it can invade the mind for no discernible reason. O God, thank you that there is nowhere I can go where you aren't waiting. No matter how low I get, you are always present with me. Even if I don't feel your presence, you have not abandoned me. Lord, I realize that sometimes you surround me with darkness so I can know the brightness of your light. The next time depression darkens my days, help me cling to the hope that I have in the light of Christ within me.

You light a lamp for me. The LORD, my God, lights up my darkness. PSALM 18:28

☼ **A prayer of LOYALTY**
How can I be a true friend?

DEAR JESUS,

Thank you for being a faithful friend. You are loyal, always available to help me in times of distress or personal struggle. Like many people, I'm often a fair-weather friend. What can I do to become more loyal? I want to be a genuine friend like you—one that stands with others in times of adversity. Show me who needs me to be a friend today.

Love never gives up, never loses faith, is always hopeful, and endures through every circumstance.
1 CORINTHIANS 13:7

DAY 56 *Prayerful Moment*

☼ **A prayer in times of WAITING**
When God answers, "Wait"

LORD,

You have promised me victory over the sin and weakness in my life, so why do I have to wait for it? Why must I still struggle after I have given my life to you? Am I not ready to handle success? Would I become too proud? Would I quickly be defeated again? Lord, please forgive my impatience. Calm my anxious thoughts. I know I can trust you as I wait, because you never waste time. Keep my heart focused on you as I wait for your perfect timing.

Be still in the presence of the LORD, and wait patiently for him to act. PSALM 37:7

☼ A prayer about SEEKING GOD
When I feel like I'm still searching for God

O LORD,

I want to be closer to you. Please create in me a desire to stay in touch with you every day, just as I stay in touch with my good friends. I invite you to go wherever I go, to see what I see, to be inside my thoughts, to share my joys and sorrows. I know you are always making that kind of effort to reach out to me, and I am so sorry for the times when I ignore you. I want to draw closer to you, for I know how much you love me. You created me. You are the source of my existence and purpose. You even know my future! No one knows more about me than you. So why don't I seek you out more often? O God, you promise that if I look for you, I will find you. As I get to know you better by spending time with you every day, I am certain I will begin to find the relationship with you that I desire. Then I'm sure I'll wonder how I ever got along without your love and guidance.

If you seek [the LORD], you will find him.
I CHRONICLES 28:9

❋ A prayer about SELF-ESTEEM
When insecurity keeps me from seeing my worth in God's eyes

DEAR JESUS,

I wrestle with insecurity. It's a part of my old sinful self that I must overcome. I can't seem to find a means to measure my worth that isn't prideful or self-debasing. I end up thinking either more highly or more poorly of myself than I should. Jesus, since you are my creator, I should look to you for an honest appraisal of my worth. In your Word, you tell me that I am valuable to you—your masterpiece. You love me deeply, and my sufficiency is in you alone. The world I live in begs me to measure my worth against its standards and to compare myself to worthless things. Please give me spiritual sight to discern when this is happening and to resist it. Instead, help me to remember that my self-esteem should be tied to the value you place on me and the purpose for which you created me. Knowing this one thing gives me hope that I can overcome my insecurities: Because I have your power within me, I am capable of doing far more than I could ever dare to dream. Thank you, Lord!

When I look at the night sky and see the work of your fingers—the moon and the stars you set in place—what are mere mortals that you should think about them, human beings that you should care for them? Yet you made them only a little lower than God and crowned them with glory and honor. PSALM 8:3-5

⚙ **A prayer about SURRENDER**
In the battles of life, when is it wise to surrender?

LORD JESUS,

In the spiritual realm I constantly fight two great battles, and surrender plays a part in both. On the one hand, I fight against sin and its control over me. If I am not allied with, I will surrender to sin and its deadly consequences. Please don't let me raise the white flag and allow sin to utterly defeat me. On the other hand, I sometimes foolishly fight against you and your will for me because I want to have ultimate control over my life. This is the battle where surrender is necessary and positive. Only when I realize how powerless I am to defeat sin will I give control of my life over to you. I must surrender. It is only when I have you, Lord, on my side that I can be victorious in my battle to defeat sin and pursue a life worth living—both now and in eternity.

Those who are dominated by the sinful nature think about sinful things, but those who are controlled by the Holy Spirit think about things that please the Spirit. So letting your sinful nature control your mind leads to death. But letting the Spirit control your mind leads to life and peace.
ROMANS 8:5-6

☼ A prayer about VULNERABILITY
When I need someone to trust with my deepest secrets

DEAR JESUS,

What if others knew who I really am? At times I am frightened by this thought, but at other times I think I might be okay with it. I really long for someone to whom I can reveal my real self: my deepest fears, hurts, sins, and doubts. Doesn't every human being need that kind of intimacy? Yet to whom could I reveal my heart? Can I trust anyone enough to be totally vulnerable with him or her? True vulnerability requires that I reveal the dark things I might have hoped would never come out in the open. While I long to be that transparent, I often resist being vulnerable about my sins, especially the ones I don't want to give up. I even do this with you, Jesus. But vulnerability requires full disclosure. It is only through being vulnerable that I will find true healing, restoration, renewal, and forgiveness. Jesus, I admit my sins. You know them already anyway. I ask for your forgiveness. I ask you to restore our relationship and take my relationships with others to an even higher position of intimacy. I want to come out of darkness and be vulnerable with you so I can receive your forgiveness, which frees me from the burdens of my sin. Thank you, God, that because of your forgiveness, I have nothing to fear. I have nothing to hide because you have changed me.

There is no condemnation for those who belong to Christ Jesus. And because you belong to him, the power of the life-giving Spirit has freed you from the power of sin that leads to death. ROMANS 8:1-2

☼ A prayer for ACCOUNTABILITY
*When I need a push to deepen my relationship
with God*

LORD,

There are some things I don't really want to ask you for.
Even though they will be good for me, I know they will
also be hard. This is one of those things. If you answer
this prayer, I know my life will be more difficult at first,
but ultimately it will be so much more satisfying. Lord,
could you please send someone to me who will force me
to open up the dark corners of my life I'd prefer to keep
hidden? May it be someone I can trust with these secrets
of the heart. I know that if I want to draw closer to you,
I am going to need someone to challenge me, to hold me
accountable for those thoughts and actions that drive a
wedge between me and you. I need that person to be firm
but loving, to care more about change in my heart than
simply my behavior. To be *un*accountable means I freely
go wherever my desires lead. My sinful nature wants that,
but my new nature in Christ knows that will lead to consequences I don't want to bear. I'd rather do the hard work
now of dealing with my sinful desires, than do the messy
work later of cleaning up after my sinful acts. I understand
it won't always be comfortable, but it's necessary. Lord,
please do what's needed and bring the right person into
my life.

You will always harvest what you plant. GALATIANS 6:7

☼ A prayer about DISCOURAGEMENT
When I'm feeling discouraged

DEAR GOD,

It's so easy to focus on my problems and forget that you are nearby and ready to help. Don't let my feelings of discouragement shake my assurance of your love for me. Discouragement causes me to doubt your love, drawing me away from my greatest source of hope. Help me to realize that you will fight on my behalf as I trust in you.

This is what the LORD says: Do not be afraid! Don't be discouraged by this mighty army, for the battle is not yours, but God's. 2 CHRONICLES 20:15

DAY 63 *Prayerful Moment*

☼ A prayer when in DOUBT
When I question what I believe

GOD,

I am encouraged when I read about the many biblical heroes who struggled with doubt. Thank you, Lord, that you're not threatened by my doubts as I seek to know you. But don't let my doubts become sin through skepticism, cynicism, or hard-heartedness. Lord, I honestly desire to understand your mysterious nature. I ask that you would bless me with a closer sense of your presence. Lead me to the truths that will strengthen my faith in you.

When doubts filled my mind, your comfort gave me renewed hope and cheer. PSALM 94:19

DAY 64

☼ A prayer of COMMITMENT
When I'm ready to count the cost of being committed to God

MY LORD AND MY GOD,

I've heard it said that I have to do "whatever it takes" if I want to be fully committed to a cause or achieve an important goal. That makes me wonder if I am doing "whatever it takes" to be your disciple. Do I truly grasp the nature of the commitment? Help me to understand the sacrifice that is needed for me to be a fully devoted follower of Jesus. Lord, I want you to be the central commitment of my life. May all other relationships and pursuits be considered in light of that. Please show me if my commitment to you is being diluted by obligations to other people, things, goals, or activities. Help me to evaluate each of my commitments by asking myself, "Is this worthy of my time and energy in light of my complete commitment to Jesus?"

If you do not carry your own cross and follow me, you cannot be my disciple. But don't begin until you count the cost. For who would begin construction of a building without first calculating the cost to see if there is enough money to finish it?
LUKE 14:27-28

☀ **A prayer about POTENTIAL**
When I long to develop into the person God created me to be

DEAR GOD,

I am created in your image, which means I have the potential to reflect your marvelous characteristics. I don't want to waste that potential! I have faith in you, God, and I give you control of my life so you can begin to develop me in the way you choose. May your Holy Spirit help me to reflect your holiness and use my spiritual gifts to help others. Help me to have an honest view of myself; I don't want to be proud because of the abilities you have given me, yet I don't want to be so self-effacing that I fail to use them for your glory. My full potential is found not in what I can do by myself, but in what you can do through me, God.

I am certain that God, who began the good work within you, will continue his work until it is finally finished on the day when Christ Jesus returns. PHILIPPIANS 1:6

☀ **A prayer about APOLOGY**
  When it's hard to say I'm sorry

DEAR GOD,

Why is it so hard for me to admit when I am wrong? Why are those two simple words, *I'm sorry*, so hard for me? I know it's pride. And I know that pride is the most dangerous of all sins, because it convinces me that I don't need you and that I know best. I need your help to work on my pride. Perhaps the best place to start is to think of those to whom I owe an apology. Apologizing requires me to realize how I have wronged someone—and then to admit it. It's so tempting to pretend my hurtful words or actions never happened, or that they were justified, or that they weren't that bad. These are signs that my heart is too proud and I am unwilling to take responsibility for my actions. When was the last time I apologized to someone? It's been too long, and that in itself is a clear indication that I need a strong dose of humility. O God, please give me the humility to say I'm sorry. Help me to long for the reconciliation, forgiveness, healing, and respect that only come from a humble heart. I confess my pride to you and ask for a heart with the courage to be able to say I'm sorry.

Always be humble and gentle. Be patient with each other, making allowance for each other's faults because of your love.
EPHESIANS 4:2

DAY 67

☼ **A prayer about the CALL OF GOD**
How can I be sure if God is calling me to do
something?

DEAR LORD,

How can I know when you are calling me to a specific
task? How can I be certain? Perhaps the first thing I need
to remember is that I don't decide when I am called—you
do. As I think about examples from the Bible, I see that
you chose *whom* you would call and *when* you would call
them. They didn't decide. At the time you chose to use
them, they were simply obeying, living faithfully for you,
and serving where you had placed them. Lord, now I see
that I don't need to worry about how you will call me.
Instead, help me to concentrate on *why* you would call
me. May I simply obey consistently, always with a humble
heart. Then if you choose to call me for a specific task, I
will be open and ready and more prepared to recognize
your instructions.

After the death of Moses the LORD's servant, the LORD spoke
to Joshua son of Nun, Moses' assistant. He said, "Moses my
servant is dead. Therefore, the time has come for you to lead
these people, the Israelites, across the Jordan River into the
land I am giving them. . . . Be strong and courageous, for
you are the one who will lead these people to possess all the
land I swore to their ancestors I would give them."
JOSHUA 1:1-2, 6

DAY 68

⚙ **A prayer for ADVICE**
  When I am looking for good advice

HEAVENLY FATHER,

What should I do now? So many times I have asked that question. In this age of conflicting claims and confusing information, where can I find wise counsel? Please lead me to those through whom you speak. And please help me to hear you when you whisper wisdom in my heart. May I seek knowledge and understanding from you—the one who knows everything that will happen today and tomorrow and every day to come. And may I learn to recognize it when you send it, through whatever means you choose to send it. Please help me to recognize my limitations and seek good counsel from the beginning, rather than discover too late that my limitations have made my problems worse. Lord, help me to avoid getting into a position where I find myself saying, "If only I had asked sooner." Thank you for your wisdom.

Get all the advice and instruction you can, so you will be wise the rest of your life. PROVERBS 19:20

A prayer about CIRCUMSTANCES
When I have trouble accepting difficult circumstances

O GOOD AND GRACIOUS GOD,

It is easy to accept the good changes that life brings, but even bad circumstances can bring spiritual growth. Teach me to accept every circumstance with thanksgiving, and to trust in your constant presence. Whether my life is sunshine or rain, you never change, Lord, and you are always eager to teach me your wisdom and truth.

Be thankful in all circumstances, for this is God's will for you who belong to Christ Jesus.
1 THESSALONIANS 5:18

DAY 70 *Prayerful Moment*

A prayer about OPPORTUNITIES
When I want to make the most of the opportunities that God puts before me

DEAR LORD,

You are the God of opportunities. Every day, you put in my path opportunities to do good. Please open my eyes so I won't miss them. I pray for the courage to be willing to respond to opportunities from you. And please teach me how to be a blessing to others as I make myself available for your work. I look forward, Lord, to what you will put in front of me today.

Make the most of every opportunity in these evil days.
EPHESIANS 5:16

☼ **A prayer about CHOICES**
When I recognize the profound responsibility of my choices

MERCIFUL GOD,

From the beginning, you have desired a loving relationship with all your people, including me. You long for me to love you in return, though in your wisdom, you knew that I must also have the freedom to choose not to follow you. In my sinful nature, I do that all too often—choosing instead to go my own way. I know this breaks your heart. Oh, how I hate when my sin drives a wedge between us. But it would be even worse if you forced people to love you—if you made us robots with no will of our own. That is surely not love, but coercion. Evil still exists, and sinful people continue to do sinful things because they choose to. But I can choose to love you. I can choose to desire a relationship with you, almighty God. With your help, I can choose to do what is right. And when I do, you draw close to me, our relationship thrives, and Satan loses ground. I look forward to the day when my sinful nature will be vanquished forever. Then I will always choose you out of the deepest desires of my heart. Until that day, help me to overcome sin by choosing to love and obey you.

The LORD God placed the man in the Garden of Eden to tend and watch over it. But the LORD God warned him, "You may freely eat the fruit of every tree in the garden— except the tree of the knowledge of good and evil. If you eat its fruit, you are sure to die." GENESIS 2:15-17

⚙ **A prayer about DISAPPROVAL**
   When I'm tempted to condemn others for their actions

DEAR JESUS,

I have sometimes pictured you as enjoying the company of only good, churchgoing people and being too holy to hang out with immoral people, but I am mistaken. When I read about you in the Bible, I learn that you found those who appeared to be the furthest from you and ministered to their needs. Following your example means looking past people's behavior to their souls. It will take the special work of your Holy Spirit to help me love those whose behaviors I disapprove of, but they are the people who most need a godly friend. My faith in you, Jesus, and my obedience to your ways shouldn't separate me from the ungodly—in fact, it qualifies me to reach out to them and serve them in love. Jesus, please show me someone I can reach out to this week.

Even the Son of Man came not to be served but to serve others and to give his life as a ransom for many.
MATTHEW 20:28

☼ A prayer about LISTENING
When I wonder if God is listening to my prayers

O GOD,

Sometimes I feel as if my prayers are bouncing off the ceiling! I don't feel like I'm getting a response, and I have to wonder, are you paying any attention? But instead of blaming you, maybe I should ask myself if I am paying attention to your response. God, you always answer prayer because you are loving and good. It's your nature to give good things to your people. How often do I pray without expecting an answer? How many times have I asked you for things but not paused to notice your response? Have I failed to give you credit because I have missed your answer to my prayers? From now on, when I pray, please alert my mind and open my eyes to notice your response, even if it isn't the one I want. Train my heart to be thankful for your answer, no matter what it is, because you have taken the time to respond to me. Thank you for the gift of prayer.

You can be sure of this: The LORD set apart the godly for himself. The LORD will answer when I call to him.
PSALM 4:3

⚙ **A prayer about the POWER OF GOD**
My testimony is evidence of God's powerful work in my life

O MIGHTY GOD,

I have experienced your power. You have helped me to conquer some areas of sin in my life that would never have been possible through my own strength. Even today, your power sustains me and protects me from backsliding into my old habits. I can say with confidence that I am your miracle. Please let my story be an encouragement to others so they may know that your power is available to them, too. Your powerful love and forgiveness are most evident to me when I see a person whose life you've redeemed, and I want to encourage others by sharing my story. At times I have had a dramatic life change, and at other times my life has been a steady walk of faith. But either way, I am a living demonstration of your powerful work within me. Lord, you receive glory when I share about your wonderful acts. May you bring me an opportunity to give you glory. And when that opportunity comes, may you give me the words to point to your powerful work in my life.

Has the LORD redeemed you? Then speak out! Tell others he has redeemed you from your enemies. PSALM 107:2

☼ A prayer about HEALING
When I am waiting for God's healing

ALMIGHTY GOD,

You made my body, and I believe you have the power to repair and restore it. You know my mind and my thoughts, and you can show me the truth. You gave me a soul, and you can bring me peace. You are not bound by the limitations of this world. You can intervene to restore any part of my life, whether in the physical, mental, spiritual, or emotional realm. I know that you love me enough to sacrifice greatly for me. You also promise that in eternity I will be fully healed. With the assurance of your love for me and the hope of your promise of ultimate healing, I have what I need to endure and wait for your healing power to make me whole—whether in this life or in eternity.

For you who fear my name, the Sun of Righteousness will rise with healing in his wings. And you will go free, leaping with joy like calves let out to pasture. MALACHI 4:2

DAY 76 *Prayerful Moment*

☼ A prayer from the HEART
When I need a change of heart

HEAVENLY FATHER,

We all reap what we sow. That is why I ask you to sow an obedient spirit in me, so that my life will produce pure thoughts, actions, and motives. Show me the roots of my rebellion, and help me to remove them from my life. Only then will my heart become soft and humble enough to receive the truth you plant there. Make my life fruitful.

Get rid of all the filth and evil in your lives, and humbly accept the word God has planted in your hearts, for it has the power to save your souls. JAMES 1:21

DAY 77 *Prayerful Moment*

☼ A prayer about DIFFERENCES
When there are people I doubt I'll ever understand

DEAR JESUS,

I fear there are people in my life with whom I will never be compatible. I don't know if we'll ever get along. But I take hope in the knowledge that, in heaven, you will restore all relationships. If you can reconcile a wolf and a lamb, how much more will you restore human relationships? I look forward to the fulfillment of your plan.

In that day the wolf and the lamb will live together; the leopard will lie down with the baby goat. The calf and the yearling will be safe with the lion, and a little child will lead them all. ISAIAH 11:6

☼ **A prayer about INITIATIVE**
When I realize how God initiated a relationship with me

DEAR GOD,

You initiated a relationship with me by giving up the life of your Son. Why doesn't this get my attention more often? It's incredible because by this act, you made it possible for me to be called your friend. I know that before Jesus died and rose again, my sins made it impossible for me to have a relationship with you. But because of your love, you made the first move. By the sacrifice you made for me, you extended your hand toward me. You offered me forgiveness before I was even born. And you give me the gift of eternity even though I could never deserve it. Thank you, Lord! The initiative you took to have a relationship with me was no token gesture. No, you went all out: a radical first move, an unthinkable sacrifice, a gift of love that could never be doubted. Because of your initiative, I know that I am precious to you and that you long for a relationship with me.

God loved the world so much that he gave his one and only Son, so that everyone who believes in him will not perish but have eternal life. JOHN 3:16

DAY 79

⚙ A prayer about LETTING GO
When I'm afraid to give anyone else control of my life

HEAVENLY FATHER,

I need to learn to let go. If could stop trying to control things, I could finally experience your best for me. Help me to know that learning to let go doesn't mean embracing a void in my life but rather aligning my mind with your plans and aligning my heart with your purposes. It is only when I give up my will that I can be filled with your will. I want to control the outcome of my efforts, but when I try, I miss the opportunity for you to work through me. After I have done my best, I need to step back and trust you to complete the work you have asked me to start. Most important, I must learn to let go to receive salvation. Out of a natural desire to control life comes the idea that I can earn my way to heaven. But salvation, heaven, and eternity come from simple belief—they are gifts. O God, teach me to let go so I can freely trust you and receive the fullness of all of your blessings to me.

I know what enthusiasm [the people of Israel] have for God, but it is misdirected zeal. For they don't understand God's way of making people right with himself. Refusing to accept God's way, they cling to their own way of getting right with God by trying to keep the law. For Christ has already accomplished the purpose for which the law was given. As a result, all who believe in him are made right with God.
ROMANS 10:2-4

☼ A prayer about CARE
When I need someone to tend to my needs

O GOD,

Your care for me is deeply personal. Your love for me began before I was born, continues throughout my life, and extends throughout eternity. You created me to have a relationship with you, and you give me the opportunity to live with you forever. Thank you! But your care for me is unique. Only you know how to love me in ways that I will respond to and that will make me feel cared for. You urge me to bring my needs and worries to you because you care so much about what happens to me. Right now, I'm struggling to find a person who seems to truly care about me. Lord, please let your love break through my feelings of loneliness and tend to my deepest needs and worries. Let me comprehend, even if just for a moment, how deeply personal your care for me really is. Thank you, God, that when no one else cares, your love never fails me.

Give all your worries and cares to God, for he cares about you.
I PETER 5:7

⚙ **A prayer about ANGER**
When I let my anger get the better of me

O LORD,

Why do I get so angry at times? It scares me sometimes because in just one moment my anger can take control of me. And most of the time, if I'm honest, it is not justified. My anger is often a bad reaction to my stubborn pride. When I am confronted because I did something wrong, I get angry. When I feel rejected, my anger button gets pushed. When I'm ignored, when I don't get my way, when I know I've let you down—there it goes again, rising up like a hot fire within me. O God, the next time anger begins to ignite within me, please help me to stop and ask, "What am I trying to protect, my pride or your honor? Am I acting out of humility or revenge?" The next time I wrong someone in my anger, help me to confess my sinful reaction. The next time I am angry, help me to forgive the one against whom I rage. The next time I am angry, help me to reconcile rather than recoil. I need your help to change, Lord. Only when your love transforms me will anger be bested.

Get rid of all bitterness, rage, anger, harsh words, and slander, as well as all types of evil behavior. Instead, be kind to each other, tenderhearted, forgiving one another, just as God through Christ has forgiven you. EPHESIANS 4:31-32

☼ **A prayer for FAITH**
When I need the courage to live by faith

DEAR LORD,

I want to have faith like the great men and women of the Bible. That means not just agreeing to a list of beliefs but being willing to stake my very life on those beliefs. When I have that kind of faith, I will be willing to trust you with my life. I will be willing to follow your guidelines for living, as outlined in the Bible, because I have the conviction that this is best for me. I will even be willing to endure ridicule and persecution for my faith because I am so sure that you are who you say you are and that you will keep your promises about salvation and eternal life. May I live every day with the certainty that you are not only the Almighty ruler of all but also the one who truly cares about who I am. With that kind of faith, I will follow wherever you lead.

It was by faith that Abraham obeyed when God called him to leave home and go to another land that God would give him as his inheritance. He went without knowing where he was going. HEBREWS 11:8

☼ A prayer about COMPATIBILITY
When my plans are in conflict with God's

DEAR GOD,

Sometimes I feel as if I'm not cut out for a life of faith. I know that I'm self-centered and that I need your Holy Spirit to change my heart and align my vision with your will. As the Spirit works in my life, I know that I will see my desires and plans begin to mirror yours. Change me, Lord, so I can enjoy the fruit of your work in my heart.

All of us who have had that veil removed can see and reflect the glory of the Lord. And the Lord—who is the Spirit— makes us more and more like him as we are changed into his glorious image. 2 CORINTHIANS 3:18

DAY 84 *Prayerful Moment*

☼ A prayer about BLESSINGS
When I want to bless others

DEAR LORD,

Help me to be a blessing to someone today. I know that blessings can be given and received; today, let me give. Grant me the opportunity to encourage, love, or comfort someone who needs a touch of your grace today. Give me discernment in both my prayers and my actions. Bring people into my path today that I can bless.

May the LORD bless you and protect you. May the LORD smile on you and be gracious to you. May the LORD show you his favor and give you his peace. NUMBERS 6:24-26

☀ **A prayer about SPIRITUAL GIFTS**
When I wonder what gifts God has given me

HEAVENLY FATHER,

I come before you with a request for instruction on my own nature. Well before I was born, you knew who I would be today; before you even laid the foundations of the world, you knew the tasks you would create me to accomplish. Help me to see myself as you do. Grant me insight into the gifts you have placed within me and the ways you want me to share them with the world. Cast my eyes on that part of me that is fashioned perfectly to do your will, bring joy to others, and share your love with this world. Please give me a passion for that part of me that delights you, and give me the courage and dedication to develop that part more fully. Guide me today toward a fuller understanding of who you have created me to be.

In his grace, God has given us different gifts for doing certain things well. So if God has given you the ability to prophesy, speak out with as much faith as God has given you. If your gift is serving others, serve them well. If you are a teacher, teach well. If your gift is to encourage others, be encouraging. If it is giving, give generously. If God has given you leadership ability, take the responsibility seriously. And if you have a gift for showing kindness to others, do it gladly.
ROMANS 12:6-8

☀ A prayer about MEMORIES
When I'm haunted by memories from my past

DEAR GOD,

It is virtually impossible for me to obey you because I am still holding on to old memories of a sinful lifestyle and longing to do the things I did before I found you. I feel like I'm trying to walk in two directions at once! God, you want me to turn away completely from the sinful habits and memories of my old life so I can experience the life you offer me. What plans of yours am I missing by allowing myself to look back at the past? When I commit myself to looking forward, with my eyes fixed on heaven, it will change the way I live. It is only by embracing your plans and my eternal future—rather than clinging to the past—that I will be able to overcome the memories that keep me from walking forward in obedience to you.

The kind of sorrow God wants us to experience leads us away from sin and results in salvation. There's no regret for that kind of sorrow. 2 CORINTHIANS 7:10

☀ A prayer for GOD'S TIMING
When I grow impatient waiting for God to act

DEAR GOD,

I am so frustrated because I have prayed and prayed, but it feels like you're not answering! What I'm asking of you seems so obviously in tune with your will, so why make me wait? I know your timing is different from mine, and I really struggle with accepting your time frame. Help me to be patient and trust that your timing will be perfect. I cannot see what is up ahead, and ultimately I want what you know is best for me. I have heard it said that you are rarely early, but you're never late. So help me to wait quietly for you to act and be confident that your way is best. When I am able to wait without becoming restless or agitated, I am trusting fully in your timing.

I wait quietly before God, for my victory comes from him. . . . Let all that I am wait quietly before God, for my hope is in him. PSALM 62:1, 5

☀ **A prayer about LETTING GO**
When I need help letting go

DEAR FATHER,

Letting go is often so hard for me. I want to be in control, but I need to learn to trust you in situations beyond my control. Teach me to do what I know is right for as long as I can and then trust you to take it from there. I know that the more I hold on to control, the less I hold on to you. I have to keep reminding myself that sometimes I serve you best by obediently standing aside and watching you work. It is only then that I realize you are the one who is really in control! I remember Moses' mother. She physically let go of her baby when she placed his basket in the water, but she did not let go of her concern for him. Because she trusted in you, you gave her the opportunity to do more for her son than she ever could have hoped for. Father, please allow me to get out of your way so that you can work like that in my life. Don't let me confuse "letting go" with "giving up." Giving up is quitting; letting go is allowing you to make the next move. May I learn this lesson in obedience and service.

Call on me when you are in trouble, and I will rescue you, and you will give me glory. PSALM 50:15

DAY 89

☀ **A prayer about ABSENCE**
   When I feel as if God is absent

MY GOD AND MY DEFENDER,

The more my troubles increase, the farther away you seem to be. Why do I feel as if you've left me in my darkest hour? I know I can't trust my feelings right now because I am lonely and overwhelmed. I need to trust in you and your promise that you will never leave me. Father, help me rely on the truth in the Bible. Let your promises reassure me that my feelings aren't true—*you* are all that's true. As I go through this treacherous journey in life, help me to remember that you are my protective shelter. Anytime I feel weary, defeated, or left behind, you are right there inviting me to come and rest in you. Even though I may not feel you walking beside me, I will seek your shelter and the comfort of your presence.

The LORD himself watches over you! The LORD stands beside you as your protective shade. PSALM 121:5

⚘ A prayer for ENERGY
When I'm tired or unenthusiastic about my work

DEAR GOD,

I'm so tired, and I feel as if I have no energy for the things I need to do each day. When I'm feeling lazy or bored with my tasks, help me to remember that I'm working for you. Infuse my labors with a sense of divine purpose so I can work with genuine enthusiasm. Help me to honor and please you in all that I do.

Work with enthusiasm, as though you were working for the Lord rather than for people. EPHESIANS 6:7

DAY 91 *Prayerful Moment*

⚘ A prayer about the HOLY SPIRIT
When I don't know what to pray for

GOD,

Sometimes I don't know how to express my heart to you. My soul longs to be recognized and understood, yet I can't find the right words. Still, I know that your Holy Spirit understands my deepest longings and expresses them to you on my behalf. I find comfort in knowing that you hear my prayers, and I am confident that you will respond.

The Holy Spirit helps us in our weakness. For example, we don't know what God wants us to pray for. But the Holy Spirit prays for us with groanings that cannot be expressed in words . . . [and] pleads for us believers in harmony with God's own will. ROMANS 8:26-27

☼ A prayer about CHILDREN
What children can teach me about trusting God

O HEAVENLY FATHER,

Thank you for the example of children. They demonstrate the kind of innocence, curiosity, and faith that is so dear to you. They approach life eager to experience new adventures and learn about the world around them, and they trust their parents to be there to guide and comfort them and meet their needs. God, the Bible tells us that you want your children to approach life the same way. You are delighted when I am willing to follow you on the adventure of life, learn all I can about you, and trust you for all I need. As an adult, I tend to make life too complicated, but you welcome me simply to trust you and anticipate with delight the blessings of divine moments with you. Teach me to put my full trust in you, for you are my Father, and I am your child.

[Jesus told his disciples,] "Let the children come to me. Don't stop them! For the Kingdom of God belongs to those who are like these children. I tell you the truth, anyone who doesn't receive the Kingdom of God like a child will never enter it."
MARK 10:14-15

☼ A prayer about THOUGHTS
When I have trouble staying focused

HOLY GOD,

I am convicted about my thought life. I waste so much time daydreaming. Too often, my mind reverts to reimagining the past or daydreaming about scenarios that might happen in the future. Either way, I am wasting the mind you gave me. I cannot change the past, so please help me not to dwell on it. I cannot control the future, so help me not to daydream or worry. I pray that you will help me focus my thoughts on the here and now. I have missed so much of your activity in the present because my mind was somewhere it shouldn't have been. O Lord, please help me to focus my thoughts back on you. Channel my thought life into things that are honorable and worthy of praise. Most important, draw my thoughts to ponder you and your mighty ways.

Dear brothers and sisters, one final thing. Fix your thoughts on what is true, and honorable, and right, and pure, and lovely, and admirable. Think about things that are excellent and worthy of praise. PHILIPPIANS 4:8

☀ A prayer for HAPPINESS
When I am looking for happiness

GOD,

Happiness comes from obeying your Word, which you gave with our best interests in mind. There was a time in my life when I ignored your Word and ran from you. I brought much unhappiness on myself by making destructive choices. It is so easy to buy into Satan's lies, thinking we have found happiness. The lies manifest themselves in so many ways: Someone craving love may choose sexual intimacy without commitment, which leads to pain and emotional scars. Someone else may believe that wealth is so important it's worth using dishonest means to acquire it. These graspings for happiness never last. But you have shown me that true happiness is cultivated by following the principles you designed for our long-term well-being. Why did I avoid your ways for so long when you graciously provide positive, healthful life principles through your Word? It is by doing what is right that I can enjoy life without fear of how it will turn out. Thank you for showing me that ultimate happiness lies in being at peace with you.

Joyful are people of integrity, who follow the instructions of the LORD. Joyful are those who obey his laws and search for him with all their hearts. They do not compromise with evil, and they walk only in his paths. PSALM 119:1-3

☼ A prayer for INTEGRITY
When I am ready to become a person of integrity

DEAR GOD,

I want to be a person of integrity. Please reveal to me how well my character is corresponding to yours. May my most important goal be to reflect the heart, mind, and actions of Jesus. Only then can I enjoy the kind of pure fellowship with you that you so desire. The more I lack integrity, the more vulnerable I am to sin and its harmful consequences. I know that integrity builds a strong wall around my heart, keeping the arrows of temptation from piercing it. Please help me to be patient, though, because I know I can't develop integrity overnight. Just as gold is made pure through a refining process that tests the metal with fire, so I am made pure through the refining process of gaining integrity. Please give me the courage to be open to how you will use the everyday circumstances of my life to refine me. Then, as my heart and actions become increasingly pure through this testing, my character will become more like yours, and I will be growing into a person of integrity.

O people, the LORD has told you what is good, and this is what he requires of you: to do what is right, to love mercy, and to walk humbly with your God. MICAH 6:8

☼ A prayer for TRUTH
When I am struggling to know what is really true

LORD,

Please give me wisdom to know what is true. So many of my friends say that truth is whatever seems right for them. But that just doesn't make sense to me. Truth has to be something that never changes, that applies to all people in all cultures over all times. That is the kind of truth I want to live by, because only that is what can come from an all-powerful, all-knowing, all-wise God. Lord, please help me to know the absolute truths you have established since the dawn of time, because then I will know how to live by your principles. And help me to know what is spiritually true—what is necessary to have a relationship with you that will mean eternal life in your presence forever. Just as I can't reject the truth about gravity and expect to function well in this world, so I can't reject the truth about how you have determined life should work and expect my future to turn out well.

Jesus told him, "I am the way, the truth, and the life. No one can come to the Father except through me." JOHN 14:6

☼ A prayer about BEAUTY
How can I learn to see God in the beauty around me?

LORD GOD,

One of the best ways to prepare my heart and mind for moments with you is simply to seek you in the beauty of your creation. The majesty of the mountains, the sound of falling rain, the smell of burning leaves on a beautiful fall day, the touch of a loved one, the taste of my favorite meal—your beauty is all around me, bombarding my senses. Help me not to become so busy or distracted that I miss those times when your beauty invades my life.

Look at the lilies and how they grow. They don't work or make their clothing, yet Solomon in all his glory was not dressed as beautifully as they are. LUKE 12:27

DAY 98 *Prayerful Moment*

☼ A prayer of SURRENDER
When I wonder why I must give my life for God

HEAVENLY FATHER,

When I surrender my life, my heart, and my desires to you, I am not left empty. In fact, you give me a new life that's far better. You fill my heart with joy and replace my old desires with new and more beautiful ones. Thank you that I receive new life by giving up my old one.

If you try to hang on to your life, you will lose it. But if you give up your life for my sake, you will save it.
MATTHEW 16:25

DAY 99

☼ **A prayer about being OVERWHELMED**
   When I'm faced with an impossible situation

ALMIGHTY GOD,

I am in the midst of a situation that requires me to do what seems impossible. I need your help! Despite the overwhelming circumstances, I thank you for encouraging me to follow you one day at a time. Please narrow my focus to the little tasks I can do today, and empower me to accomplish those so that over time, I might get through this overwhelming challenge. I will trust you to take care of what I cannot control. Thank you that this obstacle is an opportunity for you to show me your power. When I think of it that way, my circumstances don't seem so overwhelming. These hardships that frighten me are often the things that strengthen my faith the most. When I'm looking at the obstacles in my path, please remind me that there is always a little something I can do to make progress—take a small step, make a phone call, write a note, study, pray. Thank you, God, for giving me small opportunities each day to obey you so I might overcome life's obstacles through continued faithfulness.

Because the Sovereign LORD helps me, I will not be disgraced.
Therefore, I have set my face like a stone, determined to do
his will. And I know that I will not be put to shame.
ISAIAH 50:7

☼ A prayer for PASSION
When I've lost my passion for God

O DEAR LORD,

I fear I have allowed sin to dig its claws into me too deeply, and I feel as if I'm being dragged away from you. I've lost my passion for you and am feeling apathetic about spiritual things. I'm worried that Satan has me right where he wants me—with my eyes off of you and focused on something else. O Father, restore my spiritual eyesight; renew my passion for your Word. Speak to my heart as I open my Bible. Grab my attention and divert it from the sin I have fallen into. Please cultivate a thankful heart in me, for you have shown me the way of salvation! And compel my heart to engage in acts of service to others. I pray for the wisdom and courage to fight off feelings of apathy toward you and renew my passion for the purpose you have for my life. Then I will again be excited about the blessings you have given me and have promised me in the future. Glory to you, God.

Our great desire is that you will keep on loving others as long as life lasts, in order to make certain that what you hope for will come true. Then you will not become spiritually dull and indifferent. Instead, you will follow the example of those who are going to inherit God's promises because of their faith and endurance. HEBREWS 6:11-12

☼ **A prayer for DISCERNMENT**
  When life gets confusing

HEAVENLY FATHER,

Every day I am confronted with deception and lies. This world is a confusing place to travel through. Please give me a discerning mind. To follow you I need the ability to differentiate between right and wrong, true and false, good and bad, important and trivial, godly and ungodly. Help me to properly interpret the issues I'm confronted with and understand the motives of people who push a certain agenda. Show me the way through the maze of options that I face in a given day. Please give me discernment that cuts through the confusion and distractions and brings clarity to life, like the sun that burns away the fog. May I always be able to discern the direction in which you are guiding me, and may I have the courage to follow you.

Let those who are wise understand these things. Let those with discernment listen carefully. The paths of the LORD are true and right, and righteous people live by walking in them. But in those paths sinners stumble and fall.
HOSEA 14:9

DAY 102

⚙ **A prayer about EXPECTATIONS**
When I want to know what God expects of me

O LORD,

Sometimes it seems as if your expectations of me are unrealistic. How can I possibly obey all your commands? How can I love according to your standards? Humanly speaking, these expectations are impossible, but with your help they become possible. I praise you for that! By your grace, your greatest expectation is not that I live a perfect life but that I love you with all my heart. When I realize that you don't expect me to be flawless but rather are pleased when I sincerely try to follow you, I will no longer see you as a strict taskmaster but as a loving encourager. I love you, Lord.

All praise to God, the Father of our Lord Jesus Christ. It is by his great mercy that we have been born again, because God raised Jesus Christ from the dead. Now we live with great expectation, and we have a priceless inheritance— an inheritance that is kept in heaven for you, pure and undefiled, beyond the reach of change and decay.
I PETER 1:3-4

☼ **A prayer for FRIENDSHIP WITH GOD**
How can I be a friend with God?

GOD,

Because of my faith in you, you call me friend. All the qualities I look for in a friendship—honesty, loyalty, and availability—you possess perfectly. Do *I* possess the same qualities that I desire in a friend? I can be honest with you about my struggles and successes when I come to you in prayer. I can be loyal to you and your commands in the Bible. I can make myself available to walk through life with you. I look for these three qualities in my friends because I fear separation from them. I fear separation from you so much more, so I am thankful for your constant presence with me. Because you are my friend I will respect you, confide in you, and remain loyal to you.

The LORD is a friend to those who fear him. He teaches them his covenant. PSALM 25:14

✸ A prayer for ENCOURAGEMENT
I can go on because God knows my needs

MIGHTY GOD,

My world seems to be crashing down around me, and nothing is going well. The only comfort I can find is in knowing that you know exactly what I need. Sometimes I don't even know my own heart, but I'm so thankful that you are ready to meet me at my point of greatest need. Please continue to encourage me through your Word with comfort, hope, and strength.

May you experience the love of Christ, though it is too great to understand fully. Then you will be made complete with all the fullness of life and power that comes from God.
EPHESIANS 3:19

DAY 105 *Prayerful Moment*

✸ A prayer of CELEBRATION
When I feel like celebrating my faith

AWESOME GOD,

How grateful I am that you encourage us to celebrate our faith in you, to sing about you, to lift our hands in praise, to rejoice that we are saved by grace! I am so grateful to be called a child of God. May I never forget to celebrate this priceless gift and to share it with everyone I can.

Come, everyone! Clap your hands! Shout to God with joyful praise! PSALM 47:1

DAY 106

✲ **A prayer for my FUTURE**
When the future is uncertain

GOD,

From where I stand right now, the future seems scary. I don't like feeling this vulnerable, and if I'm honest, sometimes I doubt your care for me. I feel as if you are neglecting me. I don't know what will happen, and I sense the old familiar feelings of insecurity and doubt creeping into my heart and making their way into my thoughts. I've been here before, though, so I still know that you are directing my steps. Although this path may lead me through some dark valleys or seem to take some unnecessary detours, I know I will one day look back and discover that your way was perfect. You are my loving Creator, and you have always given me your best. When I consider your track record, I have no reason to doubt you in the future. Because you love me so much, why should I think that you would hold anything back? I cling to this hope for the future and wait expectantly for you to guide me to my next step.

The LORD says, "I will guide you along the best pathway for your life. I will advise you and watch over you."
PSALM 32:8

☀ **A prayer about MYSTERY**
When I contemplate the mysteries of God

ALMIGHTY GOD,

If your nature and knowledge were not beyond human understanding, you would cease to be God. My human heart longs to know you and understand all your ways. But the truth is, I can't ever claim to fully understand you. If I did, I would be making myself equal to you in my own mind. God, your mysteries are opportunities for faith. If I knew everything about you or your plans for my life, I wouldn't need faith. You have given me everything I need to know to believe in you and obey you. As I contemplate your mysterious nature, please remind me of all that you *have* chosen to reveal about who you are. You will not hold me responsible for what I don't know about you, only for what I do know—and I know that following you is a life-long adventure of discovery.

Truly, O God of Israel, our Savior, you work in mysterious ways. ISAIAH 45:15

☼ A prayer of ANTICIPATION
When I long for heaven

GOD IN HEAVEN,

You reveal just enough about your eternal home to give me something to anticipate with joy. How I long for the day when I will see and experience the place you have prepared for all believers! This anticipation encourages me to love and obey you so this life will prepare me for all you have planned in eternity. I know there is much work to be done yet on earth, and only you know when my life will come to an end and I will enter heaven. Like everyone, I dream of moments of joy and times of real rest. You have promised that these will come. Yes, God, I am eager to see what you have planned for me.

We live with great expectation, and we have a priceless inheritance—an inheritance that is kept in heaven for you, pure and undefiled, beyond the reach of change and decay. And through your faith, God is protecting you by his power until you receive this salvation, which is ready to be revealed on the last day for all to see. So be truly glad. There is wonderful joy ahead, even though you have to endure many trials for a little while. I PETER 1:3-6

☼ A prayer about WORSHIP
When I wonder if God is first in my life

DEAR GOD,

I worship you, but do I worship you alone? Or do I have idols that are really more important to me than you? What about sports, hobbies, TV, or video games? Am I more devoted to spending time with them than with you? I know that you created human beings for worship. We can't help but devote ourselves to someone or something, and we order our priorities around the object of our devotion. But your Word teaches that you alone are worthy of our worship. True worship, then, is recognizing who you are and who I am in relation to you. Ultimately, everything I do should be based on what I think of you, Almighty God, and how I worship you. If I'm not giving honor to you, then I am worshiping someone or something else. O God, may I worship only you. More than anything else, worship will connect me with you. And you are my only source of lasting hope and joy.

Shout with joy to the LORD, all the earth! Worship the LORD with gladness. Come before him, singing with joy. Acknowledge that the LORD is God! He made us, and we are his. We are his people, the sheep of his pasture. Enter his gates with thanksgiving; go into his courts with praise. Give thanks to him and praise his name. PSALM 100:1-4

☼ A prayer about CIRCUMSTANCES
When I've let my troubles rob me of my joy

DEAR GOD,

I need a change of perspective. Please teach me to focus less on my troubles and more on the joy, peace, and incredible future that come from a relationship with you. Your Word says that I can have joy despite my troubles. This means that I can always respond joyfully to you, the one who offers me the eternal gift of salvation. The more I wallow in the difficulty of unpleasant circumstances, the more they drag me under. But the more I reach out to you, the more you can lift me up. Lift me up, God! Lift up my thoughts. I pray as David prayed: "Restore to me the joy of your salvation" (Psalm 51:12).

Though the fig trees have no blossoms, and there are no grapes on the vines; even though the olive crop fails, and the fields lie empty and barren; even though the flocks die in the fields, and the cattle barns are empty, yet I will rejoice in the LORD! I will be joyful in the God of my salvation! The Sovereign LORD is my strength! He makes me as sure-footed as a deer, able to tread upon the heights.

HABAKKUK 3:17-19

☼ A prayer for my CHURCH
When I want to build up the church

DEAR JESUS,

Let the church be a place where Christian fellowship cultivates honest sharing about what really matters, encouragement to stay strong in the face of temptation and persecution, and godly wisdom for dealing with life's problems. Help us to be a powerful example of your love and faithfulness. Bless your church, and may it be a place where people can fellowship and experience your presence in a powerful way.

Let us not neglect our meeting together, as some people do, but encourage one another, especially now that the day of his return is drawing near. HEBREWS 10:25

DAY 112 *Prayerful Moment*

☼ A prayer about ETERNITY
When I long for heaven

HEAVENLY FATHER,

I am so glad for the hope I find in your promise that heaven will be something new. When you restore this earth to the way it once was—a beautiful place with no sin, sorrow, or pain—I will live in the world I long for, without evil and suffering. Most of all, I look forward to being in your presence, forever filled with joy.

Look, God's home is now among his people!
REVELATION 21:3

☼ A prayer about LEADERSHIP
When I want to be a better leader

O LORD,

Just about everyone is placed in a position to lead, be it in a family, at work, at church, or in the community. I want to be a good leader. As I strive to lead effectively, please answer these prayers: May I follow your leading. May I demonstrate godly character by example. May I delegate responsibility to trustworthy subordinates. May I courageously confront those who are doing wrong. May I lead by serving, not by giving orders. May hard times bring out the best in me. May I accept responsibility for my actions. May I consistently do the right thing. May I emphasize others' accomplishments, not my own. May I know the difference between right and wrong. May I hold myself to a higher standard of accountability. May I take good advice and act on it. May I boldly support righteousness and justice. May I always be faithful to you and rely on prayer. May my foundation be Jesus Christ. And may I be courageous knowing I have the assurance of your presence.

Jesus told them, "In this world the kings and great men lord it over their people, yet they are called 'friends of the people.' But among you it will be different. Those who are the greatest among you should take the lowest rank, and the leader should be like a servant." LUKE 22:25-26

☀ **A prayer for INSPIRATION**
  When I want my faith to inspire others

DEAR LORD,

Just as I have been inspired by others' stories of faith, may my story be an inspiration to someone today. May I not be afraid to talk about your past blessings, how I came to know you, and how you have guided me in so many ways. May I speak and act in a manner that shows my complete confidence in you and your promises to love and guide those who follow you. By remembering how you have helped me in the past, I pray that I can help others get excited about the blessings that await them in the future. Please take my simple story of faith and let it inspire someone to begin his or her own journey with you.

Commit yourselves wholeheartedly to these words of mine. Tie them to your hands and wear them on your forehead as reminders. Teach them to your children. Talk about them when you are at home and when you are on the road, when you are going to bed and when you are getting up.
DEUTERONOMY 11:18-19

⚙ **A prayer about SIGNIFICANCE**
When I feel small and insignificant

ALMIGHTY GOD,

Deep within my heart is the longing to matter. I want my life to count, to make a difference, to be worth something. Everywhere I look, I see others who are more successful, more gifted, more this, more that. No wonder I feel insignificant! I admit that often I spend far more time paralyzed by what I cannot do than acting on what I can do. My inabilities overshadow my abilities. But one of the great lessons of your Word is that the heroes of the faith—people like Moses, Gideon, Esther, and Peter—were ordinary people who learned that their significance came not from what they could accomplish with their abilities, but from what *you* could accomplish through their abilities. I am significant because I am a unique creation made in your image, almighty God. You have given me specific abilities that you want me to use for a bigger purpose. It's amazing that when I use my gifts to accomplish your work, my life becomes significant both now and for eternity.

My life is worth nothing to me unless I use it for finishing the work assigned me by the Lord Jesus—the work of telling others the Good News about the wonderful grace of God.
ACTS 20:24

☀ A prayer of HUMILITY
When I recognize the sacrifice that God has made for me

DEAR GOD,

I am humbled because I have recognized the sin in my life. Before, I was prideful, which gave the devil inroads to my heart. But now, God, in humility I want to give you my whole heart. This humility comes from sorrow over my sin as well as my recognition of the sacrifice Jesus made to free me from it. I openly admit that I need you, God, and I seek your forgiveness—something I could never have done in my proud state. I give you my whole heart and ask that you would open me up to be used for your purposes in all times and places.

He gives us even more grace to stand against such evil desires. As the Scriptures say, "God opposes the proud but favors the humble." So humble yourselves before God. Resist the devil, and he will flee from you. Come close to God, and God will come close to you. Wash your hands, you sinners; purify your hearts, for your loyalty is divided between God and the world. Let there be tears for what you have done. . . . Humble yourselves before the Lord, and he will lift you up in honor. JAMES 4:6-10

☼ **A prayer about UNITY**
  When I wonder if real unity is possible

DEAR JESUS,

Why am I so quick to judge others who are different rather than embracing and celebrating their differences? Why am I intimidated by anyone who doesn't share my opinion? Your Word says that each person is unique, so I shouldn't be surprised by differences of opinion. In fact, because your Word emphasizes unity within the church, our differences must serve some important goal. Please teach me how to embrace different people and opinions for the sake of a shared goal. I know that I often hinder unity because I'm so convinced that my ideas are best. This mind-set keeps me from listening to new opinions that might actually inform my own for the better. Jesus, teach me to celebrate others' differences. Open my heart and soften it toward others. I long to experience the true unity you designed humans to share and enjoy.

You are all children of God through faith in Christ Jesus. And all who have been united with Christ in baptism have put on Christ, like putting on new clothes. There is no longer Jew or Gentile, slave or free, male and female. For you are all one in Christ Jesus. GALATIANS 3:26-28

☀ **A prayer in time of SORROW**
When the sorrow is overwhelming

MY HEAVENLY FATHER,

Draw near me in my moment of sorrow. What I have lost can never be regained, and I sense part of me will never be the same. Enter my darkness, Lord, and fill this room with your holy presence. Please be patient with me, Lord. Sit with me now in my time of grief, and comfort me with your presence. Comfort me while I shed my tears. I need you near me.

Weeping may last through the night, but joy comes with the morning. PSALM 30:5

DAY 119 *Prayerful Moment*

☀ **A prayer for my ENEMIES**
When I need God's supernatural power to love my enemies

DEAR LOVING FATHER,

Showing love to my enemies seems completely unreasonable—until I realize that I was once *your* enemy, and then you forgave me. Help me to see my enemies as you see them—as people in need of grace and forgiveness. May I feel compassion for them; may I extend love and mercy and forgiveness, as you have done for me.

You have heard the law that says, "Love your neighbor" and hate your enemy. But I say, love your enemies! Pray for those who persecute you! MATTHEW 5:43-44

☼ A prayer for WISDOM
When I wonder where to find wisdom

DEAR GOD,

I'd like to think I'm an intelligent person, but I still face situations in life that I don't have the wisdom to navigate. I'm learning that success in relationships, fulfillment of my life's purpose, and spiritual maturity are often more dependent on wisdom than on intellect. Wisdom is what transforms head knowledge into discernment. Your Word says that wisdom grows out of knowledge of you and respect for your commands. God, please reveal your wisdom to me through your Word. Forgive the pride I take in my own mental abilities, and help me not to rely on my own intelligence. Your Word tells me that only those with humble and teachable hearts who are committed to steady obedience will absorb the wisdom found in you. I want to do that, Lord! Help me to remember that wisdom is less about knowing facts and more about knowing you.

Fear of the LORD is the foundation of wisdom. Knowledge of the Holy One results in good judgment. PROVERBS 9:10

☼ **A prayer for COMFORT**
In times of distress, how can I experience God's comfort?

GOD IN HEAVEN,

You don't always act in the way I might expect, and that is a blessing. I sometimes expect you to comfort me by providing things that I want or need; instead, you often reassure me with your presence. How awesome that your comfort is so personal. Things are temporary, but you are eternal. My needs and wants are constantly changing, so material provisions can provide comfort only for a time. But you, God, are the only source of comfort at all times. I am so grateful that every time I need comfort, you show up—not with presents, but with your abiding presence.

I know the LORD is always with me. I will not be shaken, for he is right beside me. . . . You will show me the way of life, granting me the joy of your presence and the pleasures of living with you forever. PSALM 16:8, 11

☼ A prayer of REPENTANCE
When I need my life to go a different direction

DEAR JESUS,

Just like a car going the wrong way on a one-way street, I've been traveling the wrong direction with my life. I have not been going your way, but the way of sin. It's time to make a U-turn and change course as fast as I can before disaster strikes. Lord Jesus, I repent of my sin. I want to turn from my sinful way and follow your way. I admit that my sin has caused me to move away from you. I am making a commitment now, with your help, to change the direction of my life. Some people say I should do whatever I want, and others want to call my sinful way of life nothing more than a little mistake. But I know it is sin. I have not been living the way you created me to live, and that means I have been rebelling against you. Please forgive me. I want to repent fully—to change my course and move toward you instead of away from you. May I keep going now in the right direction.

Repent of your sins and turn to God, so that your sins may be wiped away. ACTS 3:19

DAY 123

☼ **A prayer for CHANGE**
  Why does godly transformation take so long?

DEAR JESUS,

I am your work of art—and one that's definitely still in process. Why does it take such a long time for you to complete your work in me? In this moment I am fervent in my faith, inspired to change. But I know being transformed into godliness takes a lifetime. For real and dynamic change to occur, you have to give me a new heart and a new way of thinking. So I ask you to make the change in me. May the Holy Spirit help me to focus on what is true and good and right. How I long to see the new me—a person who displays your goodness and holiness! When these changes seem to be coming slowly, remind me that your work in me is relentless and certain. Please give me patience with myself as I trust you to work in me at just the right pace.

Anyone who belongs to Christ has become a new person.
The old life is gone; a new life has begun!
2 CORINTHIANS 5:17

☼ A prayer for RESPECT
Where can I find respect?

LORD,

I want to be respected, but I think I'm going about it the wrong way. Among some of my friends, the person who is the most wealthy, most beautiful, most popular, or most self-serving gains the admiration of the group. It's a competition. But the more I strive to gain others' approval, the less self-respect I have. And the esteem I gain is a mirage— it only lasts until someone else outdoes me. I need a new approach, Lord. I'm starting to learn that earning respect doesn't come from serving myself but from serving others, from taking responsibility instead of trying to save face. The people I genuinely look up to show consistent kindness and integrity and are motivated by a deep love for others. Their self-respect comes from knowing whom they serve, and others admire them for their consistently godly lives. Father, I don't want to make other people feel that they are less important than I am. I want to be respected because people see more of you in me. Please answer my prayer for change. Only you can help me become the kind of person who truly deserves respect.

He must become greater and greater, and I must become less and less. JOHN 3:30

☼ A prayer about COMMITMENT
How can I motivate others to greater commitment?

DEAR GOD,

Today, I dedicate myself to you so that others may see in my life a contagious commitment. May I serve you today out of passionate love and devotion, so much that those around me can't help but see you in me. May I be so pre-occupied with you that my words and deeds are an accurate reflection of your grace and your truth and your love.

Jesus replied, "'You must love the LORD your God with all your heart, all your soul, and all your mind.' This is the first and greatest commandment. A second is equally important: 'Love your neighbor as yourself.'" MATTHEW 22:37-39

DAY 126 *Prayerful Moment*

☼ A prayer for FAITH
When I want to strengthen my faith

DEAR GOD,

Strengthen my faith and sharpen my spiritual vision so that I can sense your work in my life. Help me to see in the spiritual realm what you are doing in the world. Open my eyes to the transforming power of your Spirit, and help me to see how you are able to work through my life today.

Faith is the confidence that what we hope for will actually happen. HEBREWS 11:1

☼ **A prayer about PURPOSE**
When I want to understand God's plans

DEAR GOD,

Understanding the deep truths that help life make sense doesn't come easily. I must search for understanding. I must *want* to know why you made me and what you want me to do. But you haven't left me without a way to find out. God, you have left believers an entire book—the Bible—and you told us to read it before you return, because it tells us exactly what we need to know to have a purposeful life. As I read your Word, I pray that you would answer my desire to know you—your character and your commands. And as I seek to know your plans, I pray that you would reveal to me the way of righteous living. I pray for understanding so that I can say with confidence, "My God has plans for me!"

All Scripture is inspired by God and is useful to teach us what is true. . . . God uses it to prepare and equip his people to do every good work. 2 TIMOTHY 3:16-17

☀ A prayer about SERVICE
When I want to serve God effectively

GOD,

I want to be an effective servant for you because it is a privilege to belong to you. It gives me great joy to be part of your family and to have the opportunity to extend your love to others, as others extended it to me. I pray that you will always sustain this joy and reverent awe so I will not become dull in my service to you. I desire to please you and obey your Word. Don't let me wander from your commandments, because it is through obedience that I can be the best example of your love to others. Help me to accept that sometimes I must sacrifice my own comfort and desires to reach out to those who need it most. Let me show my devotion to you by putting others first. Finally, Lord, please fill me with a genuine love for you and for others that will compel me to serve authentically. Please bless my desire to love and serve you faithfully all the days of my life.

You have been called to live in freedom, my brothers and sisters. But don't use your freedom to satisfy your sinful nature. Instead, use your freedom to serve one another in love. GALATIANS 5:13

DAY 129

☼ A prayer about MENTORING
Should I be mentoring someone?

LORD,

Should I be exploring a one-on-one mentoring relationship with someone who is younger? Should I be sharing
the wisdom and life experiences I have gleaned over the
years to help a younger person learn? I am so grateful for
the older people who shared stories from their lives, helping me grow into the kind of person I am now. I sense you
are encouraging me to do the same. I don't have much
to offer, but my experiences might be helpful to someone just beginning his or her adult life. Who might I help
and encourage spiritually? I want to be a part of causing
faith to continue from generation to generation and helping younger people learn how to live effectively for you.
If there are those I can help, O Lord, please send them to
me. Then please grant me the wisdom to teach them how
to grow in their relationship with you.

*You have heard me teach things that have been confirmed
by many reliable witnesses. Now teach these truths to other
trustworthy people who will be able to pass them on to
others.* 2 TIMOTHY 2:2

☼ A prayer about ATTITUDE
When I need a new outlook on my problems

FATHER,

You are famous for creating something out of nothing. What I see as rubble and wasteland in my own life are the raw materials for your restoration and redemption. Sometimes only this thought helps me maintain a positive attitude through my struggles. It is easy to become bitter, cynical, or even hopeless when life throws hard times my way. But I know, God, that you see them as a crucible refining me and strengthening my character and convictions. Hard times can be your way of turning the raw materials of my life into something useful for you. I can be confident of this because your Word tells me that when I was nobody, a helpless sinner, Jesus died because you saw me as someone created in your image for a purpose. You have already transformed nothing into something in my life, and I praise you for it. Help me to see my problems as opportunities for you to do what you do best!

If we are to share [Christ's] glory, we must also share his suffering. Yet what we suffer now is nothing compared to the glory he will reveal to us later. ROMANS 8:17-18

☼ **A prayer about HELP**
When I'm reluctant to ask for help

DEAR GOD,

I know I have limitations. I struggle with areas of weakness, experience feelings of inadequacy, and lack skills and abilities I wish I had. So often my limitations keep me from knowing what to do or how to do it—and when that happens, I resist asking for assistance. But I must acknowledge that I need help. Our culture admires the strong, independent spirit, but the truth is that no one can really survive alone. That's why you created us to be in relationship with you and other people, and that means giving and receiving help. I need help to get work done. I need help to restore relationships. I need help to develop skills. I need help to think through my problems. And I really need help to say I'm sorry. I am going to start by asking you for help right now. You are my greatest helper, for you are wiser, stronger, and more loving than anyone on earth. Please show me how to cultivate the habit of seeking help from others and from you. I want to experience those moments when you come to my rescue. And may you use me to come to the rescue of others. May I not be afraid to offer help to those in need, even though I feel inadequate. I'll give you the glory, Lord.

The LORD is my strength and shield. I trust him with all my heart. He helps me, and my heart is filled with joy.
PSALM 28:7

☼ A prayer about SPIRITUAL WARFARE
When I sense spiritual attack

LORD OF HEAVEN'S ARMIES,

The Bible clearly teaches that human beings are involved in a spiritual battle. As one of your followers, I am right in the middle of the war. Equip me for the battle, Lord. Arm me with spiritual power and wisdom, and help me to resist the evil one and to flee from temptation. Grant me victory, Lord, as you have promised.

We are not fighting against flesh-and-blood enemies, but against evil rulers and authorities of the unseen world, against mighty powers in this dark world, and against evil spirits in the heavenly places. EPHESIANS 6:12

DAY 133 *Prayerful Moment*

☼ A prayer about COMPETITION
When I seek success for the wrong reasons

JESUS,

I confess that my competitive nature and my desire for success can cause me to focus on pursuing my own goals. But I know that without you, Lord, I'll never achieve anything of lasting value. Help me to channel my competitive nature into pursuing things that will last for eternity.

Whatever I am now, it is all because God poured out his special favor on me. . . . Yet it was not I but God who was working through me by his grace.
I CORINTHIANS 15:10

⚙ **A prayer about STUBBORNNESS**
How do I know when I am being stubborn?

DEAR GOD,

Please reveal to me where my stubbornness is choking out my faith. I know that sometimes I am so set in my ways that I'm not convinced you can change me. May I always believe that you can make a difference in my life. May I never let difficult circumstances convince me that you do not care. May I never stop praying because I've made up my mind it won't help. May I never refuse to trust you. Open my spiritual eyes so I can see clearly that following your way of living, as found in the Bible, will make my life better both now and for eternity. Give me confidence that your plan for my life is actually better than mine. O God, break through my stubbornness. Show me how to give up those things I think are so good and exchange them for things you know are so much better. And when I learn to trust you fully and let go of my own plans, I will find myself giving the glory to you rather than to me.

Be careful then, dear brothers and sisters. Make sure that your own hearts are not evil and unbelieving, turning you away from the living God. You must warn each other every day, while it is still "today," so that none of you will be deceived by sin and hardened against God. For if we are faithful to the end, trusting God just as firmly as when we first believed, we will share in all that belongs to Christ.

HEBREWS 3:12-14

⚙ **A prayer of STEWARDSHIP**
When I need to be a better steward of what I have

O FATHER,

Thank you for all that you have entrusted into my care. You have given me responsibility for people and for things, and I want to be a good steward. If I made a list of my stewardship responsibilities, it would get quite long: my financial resources and material possessions; my talents and time; the people under my care such as my family, Sunday school class, or the care group I lead. I ask you, O God, how I can better manage these assets you have given me. Help me to see that the goal of stewardship is to make the best possible use of what you have entrusted to me in order to make the greatest possible impact on others. I want your work to move forward as effectively as possible. Please show me today where I need to be a better steward.

The master was full of praise. "Well done, my good and faithful servant. You have been faithful in handling this small amount, so now I will give you many more responsibilities. Let's celebrate together!" MATTHEW 25:21

DAY 136

☼ A prayer for SIMPLICITY
When life becomes too complicated

JESUS,

My life feels cluttered. Not just with material things, but with my own distracted thoughts and desires. I wish that things were simpler—not just my lifestyle, but the inner attitude of my heart. I know it's time to return to simplicity when I stop being thankful and start feeling entitled; when I begin grasping for everything in sight rather than trusting you to provide; when I hold on desperately to what I own instead of sharing it with those around me. Jesus, help me to be thankful—viewing every possession and good occurrence as a gift from you so I get to the place where I expect nothing but am delighted with everything. Help me to trust that my life is ultimately under your care. Free me from feeling as if I have to own everything, because the truth is, all things belong to you. Help me to be generous—willing to share all I have with others as an expression of your generosity to me. Restore in me a thankful, trusting, generous spirit so I can live simply.

This world is fading away, along with everything that people crave. But anyone who does what pleases God will live forever. 1 JOHN 2:17

⚙ **A prayer for FELLOWSHIP**
When I am grateful for Christian friendships

DEAR LORD,

Thank you for the unique bond that brings believers in Jesus together. Thank you for my church, for Christian fellowship, for how we care for one another. This bond of fellowship is unique because it invites the living God into our midst and offers supernatural help in dealing with our problems. We have a common perspective on life because we know our sins have been forgiven, we have experienced the joy of salvation, and we know we have a future together in heaven. How encouraging that our gatherings provide a place for honest sharing about the things that really matter in life, and encouragement to stay strong in the face of temptation. Lord, I know that Christian fellowship is a good thing, for we help each other stay strong in our faith, and we encourage, comfort, warn, and bless each other. Thank you for the wonderful gift of fellow believers.

When we get together, I want to encourage you in your faith, but I also want to be encouraged by yours. ROMANS 1:12

☼ A prayer about SUCCESS
When I need a better definition of success

MY LORD AND FRIEND,

If I were to reach the end of life having managed a successful business, raised a nice family, won all kinds of community awards, and retired comfortably, would you say my life had been a success? No, if I did all those things apart from you, I believe you would say my life had been a failure. Failure in your eyes is not living the way you created me to live—in other words, not living in relationship with you. If I died today, would you say I had done that? My greatest failure would be to reject you, because apart from you, nothing will ultimately last. Please don't allow me to fail by neglecting or ignoring you, O loving Father. You know the secret to successful life; you created it! Therefore I will fail if I go against you and try to find my own path. But I will succeed if I discover what a relationship with you now means for all eternity. Please guide me toward that success, Lord.

What do you benefit if you gain the whole world but lose your own soul? Is anything worth more than your soul?
MATTHEW 16:26

✹ A prayer about PRETENDING
When I want my faith to be more genuine

DEAR GOD,

Help me to care more about other people. I don't want to only pretend to care about the needy, or pretend not to notice when someone needs help, or pretend there's nothing I can do. Please change my heart so that I really care—just like you do. May my faith become genuine and active, ready to go the extra mile to help those in need.

Dear children, let's not merely say that we love each other; let us show the truth by our actions. Our actions will show that we belong to the truth, so we will be confident when we stand before God. 1 JOHN 3:18-19

DAY 140 *Prayerful Moment*

✹ A prayer of HOSPITALITY
When I want my home to be an inviting place

DEAR JESUS,

When people enter my home, I do all I can to make them feel welcome and wanted. But sometimes I get caught up with the cleanliness and condition of my house and I don't want to have people in. Give me a true spirit of hospitality that focuses on people and not on peripherals. Make my home an example of your grace and a foretaste of the hospitality we'll enjoy in heaven.

This world is not our permanent home; we are looking forward to a home yet to come. HEBREWS 13:14

DAY 141

☼ **A prayer of OBEDIENCE**
Wisdom comes from abiding by God's perfect commands

HEAVENLY FATHER,

The Bible tells me that obedience to your commands brings wisdom. In other words, the right thing to do is the smart thing to do. Your commandments are not burdensome obligations but pathways to a joyful, meaningful, and satisfying life. Your call to obedience comes from your own commitment to my well-being. Since you are the creator of life, you know the best way to live. God, please point out those areas in my life where I am not living your best for me. Let me see where I have settled for something good instead of seeking your perfect plan. Show me where I have fallen short of the abundant life you have intended for me, and challenge me to restore my life to obedience in these areas. Make me willing to accept your commandments and trust in your ways. Plant a love for your commands in my heart so I may be wise and obedient to you.

God is working in you, giving you the desire and the power to do what pleases him. PHILIPPIANS 2:13

☀ A prayer about PAIN
When I need divine comfort in my pain

DEAR JESUS,

Whether it comes from betrayal, neglect, abandonment, or from a broken bone or failing health—the result is some kind of emotional or physical pain. When I look back on my life, I remember the physical tension of my aching body or the chest-tightening ache that came from a broken heart. My greatest hope in times of pain is that you will bring me healing. Thank you that I never have to worry you haven't noticed my pain. How compassionate you are to comfort me in my hurts. On the other hand, there are times when I hurt so badly that I forget about you, Jesus. I become completely focused on how to stop the pain. But you never abandon me. When I feel alone in my hurt, it is often because I am concentrating so much on easing the pain of my problems that I have forgotten you have promised to help me in my difficulties. Thank you that you never leave me. I find comfort in your promise to be with me and give me hope and purpose in the midst of my aching body and soul.

We believers also groan, even though we have the Holy Spirit within us as a foretaste of future glory, for we long for our bodies to be released from sin and suffering. We, too, wait with eager hope for the day when God will give us our full rights as his adopted children, including the new bodies he has promised us. We were given this hope when we were saved. ROMANS 8:23-24

DAY 143

⚙ **A prayer about VALUE**
When I feel like I can't do anything right

DEAR GOD,

I'm down on myself right now. I put on a good front, but I don't feel very competent in my work, my relationships, as a spouse, or as a parent. It seems as if someone is always disappointed in me. And when I do accomplish something, I see ten other people who can do it better and I say, "Why bother?" I know I'm focusing too much on myself again, Lord. This is why I come to you in prayer. I need to remember that I am priceless to you because you love me. The God of the universe loves me! That makes me a person of great value indeed. Please keep me from measuring myself by the wrong standards. How I compare to others isn't important. The only thing that matters—and the only way to avoid my insecurities—is to find my value as a creation of almighty God. When I reflect on how much you love me, I find the courage to be myself, and I realize I might be more valuable than I give myself credit for.

We are God's masterpiece. He has created us anew in Christ Jesus, so we can do the good things he planned for us long ago.
EPHESIANS 2:10

⚙ **A prayer for OBEDIENCE**
When I struggle with the concept of obedience

O GOD,
Obedience is difficult for me. May I not see it as simply a set of rules or standards of behavior. Instead, may I see how obedience actually frees me to enjoy life as you intended because it keeps me from becoming entangled in harmful situations. I must admit that your commandments are sometimes difficult to obey or don't always make sense from my human perspective, but I will trust that obedience to you will bring blessing, joy, and peace. When I look at obedience this way, I will desire to obey you out of love and gratitude for all you are trying to do for me rather than out of fear of being punished. The more I obey out of love, the more I will *want* to obey, and the more obedience will become a lifestyle rather than a chore. O God, you are the creator of life, so only you know how life is supposed to work. You say obedience works. May my obedience demonstrate my trust that your way is best, and that it will work for me.

If you look carefully into the perfect law that sets you free,
and if you do what it says and don't forget what you heard,
then God will bless you for doing it. JAMES 1:25

DAY 145

⚙ **A prayer of RESPONSIBILITY**
*When I need to take more responsibility for
my actions*

DEAR GOD,

I've always been taught that a bad habit is something I impose on myself, like smoking, drinking, or taking drugs. But you're beginning to show me that things like spreading gossip, complaining, backbiting, and even worry are bad habits too. One of Satan's great lies is that I am a victim who has no power to resist my impulses and therefore I don't have to take responsibility for my choices and actions. But in reality, everything I do is the result of a choice I make—and I am responsible for every choice. It's hard to resist every temptation and always make good choices. O God, please break the chains that hold me and give me self-control. Your Word promises that you are more powerful than anything that controls me. Please give me the boldness to take responsibility for that first step away from my bad habits, and please be with me every step of the way through the power of your Holy Spirit.

*Don't you realize that you become the slave of whatever
you choose to obey? You can be a slave to sin, which leads to
death, or you can choose to obey God, which leads to righteous living.* ROMANS 6:16

☼ A prayer when I'm TIRED
When I'm weary and in need of renewal

DEAR GOD,

Thank you that you renew my strength when I grow weary. Thank you for refreshing my heart when I come to you in praise. Thank you for refreshing my soul when I come to you in prayer. Thank you for refreshing my mind when I come to you in meditation. Thank you for refreshing my body when I come to you in solitude. And thank you for refreshing my perspective on life when I come to you with thankfulness. Thank you that I can draw strength from you, the source of all strength.

Jesus said, "Come to me, all of you who are weary and carry heavy burdens, and I will give you rest." MATTHEW 11:28

DAY 147 *Prayerful Moment*

☼ A prayer about BUSYNESS
When I am busy all the time and accomplish so little

O GOD,

I often operate under the false assumption that being busy means being productive, or that resting is synonymous with laziness. Help me to see that it's possible to have unproductive activity and productive rest. Teach me, Lord, to strike a balance between working, celebrating, and resting so that I may be productive in all areas of life.

He lets me rest in green meadows; he leads me beside peaceful streams. PSALM 23:2

☼ A prayer for VICTORY
When I want to live a more victorious Christian life

O GOD ALMIGHTY,

How I thank you that my greatest victory was won when I received salvation through the death and resurrection of Jesus. Because he conquered death, I will too. Glory to you, God! But even after that victory I still need your help, Lord, for the daily battles over the strongholds of sin that threaten my ability to effectively live the Christian life. I need daily victories over sin, for it still seeks to destroy my witness and my purpose. Don't allow sin to harass me, but help me overcome its daily attacks. I want to live a victorious life. So step by step, victory by victory, help me battle relentlessly against sin and remove it from my heart piece by piece. Because I trust you and you live in me, I praise you that you have equipped me with everything I need to accomplish this.

They will fight against you like an attacking army, but I will make you as secure as a fortified wall of bronze. They will not conquer you, for I am with you to protect and rescue you. I, the LORD, have spoken! JEREMIAH 15:20

⚙ **A prayer for JOY**
When I want something more than happiness

O LORD,

Help me to grasp the difference between joy and happiness. I want to be happy, just like everyone else, but I realize that happiness is a temporary reaction to events in my life. Instead, create in me a greater desire for joy, which is strong and lasting, and can happen in spite of my circumstances. This kind of joy comes by following you and living according to your principles. If happiness is all I can count on, I will always need to experience happy events to keep me going. But with joy, I know that no matter what happens, you offer hope and promise. Joy is celebrating my walk with you, O God. It is having peace with you. It is realizing how privileged I am to know Jesus as my Savior, to have my sins forgiven, to be friends with you, God Almighty. It is experiencing the dramatic change that occurs when I allow the Holy Spirit to control my heart and mind. You do not promise constant happiness, but you do promise lasting joy to those who follow you. Thank you, Lord.

Since we have been made right in God's sight by faith, we have peace with God because of what Jesus Christ our Lord has done for us. Because of our faith, Christ has brought us into this place of undeserved privilege where we now stand, and we confidently and joyfully look forward to sharing God's glory. ROMANS 5:1-2

☼ A prayer in times of DEPRESSION
When I feel low following a spiritual victory

O GOD,

How can I be experiencing such deep discouragement just months after being on such a spiritual high? I felt so close to you—I had experienced great victory in my relationship with you—and now I feel so far away. But if I'm being honest, I know the reason. When I was on top of the world, I didn't seem to need you as much. I neglected you. No wonder I now feel distant. We haven't talked, really talked, in a long time. O God, how I need you. Come to me in my discouragement. May I fill my heart and mind with your Word, which will encourage me with your love. Recognizing your love and care once again will begin to pull me up from the mire of my depression.

He lifted me out of the pit of despair, out of the mud and the mire. He set my feet on solid ground and steadied me as I walked along. PSALM 40:2

⚙ A prayer for RENEWAL

When my life is a mess and I need a fresh start

DEAR GOD,

How often I am disappointed with myself. I have such high hopes and good intentions, but inevitably I find myself weary and burned out with self-defeat, the burdens of everyday living, or the consequences of bad choices and sinful actions. The messiness of life can leave me feeling exhausted—not only physically but also in my very soul. If only I could start over. Isn't this the place where renewal begins? Your compassion and my ready heart meet to bring about change. When the two are put together, I find a new beginning where my soul is refreshed and my life revived. You make it clear that you will restore any heart that seeks a new start. I sincerely desire to turn to you and turn away from what has been bringing me down. I ask you to forgive my sin, which poisons everything I do. Thank you that I am never beyond the reach of your forgiveness as long as I desire it. My heart is truly ready to change. Please renew my life with the change that only your Spirit can bring.

Create in me a clean heart, O God. Renew a loyal spirit within me. PSALM 51:10

☼ A prayer for GRACE
How do I receive God's grace?

LORD GOD,

When the Bible says I am saved by grace, it means that you have done me the biggest favor of all—you have pardoned me from the death sentence I deserve because of my sins. I do not have to earn your favor or work my way into heaven. By grace I am forgiven for my sins and restored to full fellowship with you. Thank you, Lord. Please let me be humble enough to recognize my need for you and to request your forgiveness. The more I realize how much I need your grace, the more I realize I don't deserve it—which is exactly why I need it! I cannot take credit for my salvation any more than a baby can brag about being born. The fact that this is your gift and not the product of my own effort gives me great comfort, security, and hope. Help me to accept your grace like the gift it is.

God saved you by his grace when you believed. And you can't take credit for this; it is a gift from God. Salvation is not a reward for the good things we have done, so none of us can boast about it. EPHESIANS 2:8-9

☼ A prayer of ACCEPTANCE
When my circumstances are difficult to accept

O LORD,

In this fallen world, help me to have realistic expectations about my earthly home. Prepare me for troubles that are sure to come. Remind me that I can accept my circumstances without liking them. Help me to be heaven-minded so that I can grow through adversity, knowing that these difficulties will end with this earthly life. I accept whatever comes from your hand, and I trust your wisdom.

What we suffer now is nothing compared to the glory he will reveal to us later. ROMANS 8:18

DAY 154 *Prayerful Moment*

☼ A prayer about CHURCH
When the church needs me

DEAR GOD,

Thank you for giving every believer special gifts. When your people use their gifts to serve, the church becomes a powerful force for good, a strong witness for you, and a mighty army to combat Satan's attacks. I am humbled to be a part of such an important group. Lord, help me to use my gifts to support the body of Christ.

Just as our bodies have many parts and each part has a special function, so it is with Christ's body. We are many parts of one body, and we all belong to each other.
ROMANS 12:4-5

⚙ **A prayer about FORGIVENESS**
When I have trouble believing God will forgive me

O GRACIOUS GOD,

You are the one who has ultimately been wronged by my sin, so I come to seek forgiveness from you first. Oh, how I thank you that your forgiveness is not based on the magnitude of my sin but on the magnitude of the forgiver's love. And so I confess my sin to you as the first step in receiving your forgiveness. I have done something wrong, but because your Son, Jesus, died on the cross to take the punishment for my sin and rose from the dead to show his power over death, you accept my confession and forgive me. There is nothing more I must do. It is too wonderful to believe! When you forgive me, you look at me as though I have never sinned; I become blameless before you. How can that be? Yet you say it is true. Please don't allow lingering feelings of shame to persuade me otherwise. How I thank you that nothing I've done in my past is so bad that your complete and unconditional love can't forgive it. Only those who don't want your forgiveness are out of its reach. To you, God, be the glory!

He has reconciled you to himself through the death of Christ. . . . As a result, he has brought you into his own presence, and you are holy and blameless as you stand before him without a single fault. COLOSSIANS 1:22

☼ A prayer about FLEXIBILITY
When I'm inflexible with my plans for my life

DEAR LORD,

I find it very difficult to be flexible. I like control and order, and I always have a plan. But God, my spiritual walk seems to have come to a stop. I wonder if my plans have come to a dead end. I need a change. I need to be more flexible. First, God, I ask that you would help me evaluate my life to see if there is anything that I follow more closely than you. Even if it is an important part of my plan or daily life, I pray that you would help me to leave it behind and devote myself to you with all my heart. Second, help me to seek your timing and allow room in my life to change my plans. Wherever I am, whatever I do, I can do it with an attitude of service to you. Let me be eager to leave my plans and adopt yours. O God, I want to be flexible so my spiritual walk can commence once again. Prepare my heart for surprise moments with you as you guide me through life.

As soon as they landed, they left everything and followed Jesus. LUKE 5:11

☼ A prayer for REST
When the treadmill of life leaves me exhausted

O LORD,

My world of perpetual motion creates a life of anxiety and stress. I sometimes actually take pride in telling others how busy I am, and I feel guilty if I stop to relax. But you did not intend for people to live in a state of frenzied activity. From your own example when you worked to create the earth, it is clear that you want us to have refreshment for body and soul. Why would the omnipotent God of the universe rest after doing the work of creation? Surely it wasn't because you, the Almighty, were tired! The answer I see, O God, is that you, in ceasing from your work, proclaimed rest to be holy. You created us in such a way that we would need to stop our work to care for our physical and spiritual needs. I know work is good and brings so many benefits to my life. But I also know you want my work to be balanced with regular rest and attention to my physical and spiritual health. Otherwise, I will lack energy and miss precious moments of quiet time with you. Lord, teach me how to rest.

The LORD is my shepherd; I have all that I need. He lets me rest in green meadows; he leads me beside peaceful streams. He renews my strength. He guides me along right paths, bringing honor to his name. PSALM 23:1-3

☀ **A prayer about DESIRES**
When I need insight into my own desires

LORD GOD,

I need discernment. There is something I want, and I just can't stop thinking about it. I don't know if what I desire is good or bad, but it is constantly in my thoughts. I'm feeling so confused. Please, meet me in this moment with the insight I need. You know all things, even the deep recesses of my heart. You know what the long-term outcome of my choice will be. O God, please shine your light on this desire. If it is wrong, expose it for the foolishness that it is. But if my motives are pure, then affirm me in my spirit. Either way, I need to be at peace with you! You are my counselor and my friend. I trust that you will show me the truth about what I desire.

The LORD is close to all who call on him, yes, to all who call on him in truth. He grants the desires of those who fear him; he hears their cries for help and rescues them.
PSALM 145:18-19

☼ A prayer about CRITICISM
When I need to offer constructive criticism

DEAR GOD,

I don't like criticism, even when it is constructive, but sometimes I need it. Help me to welcome constructive criticism so that I can become more like the person you created me to be. It is much easier to receive someone else's assessment when it is offered gently and in love rather than in a harsh or humiliating way. Please remind me to offer criticism the same way I would like to receive it. I don't want to judge; that is evaluating others with no intent to see them improve. When I offer constructive criticism, may my goal be to help that person become who you created him or her to be. When I must criticize, may it not be a discouraging experience in that person's life but rather a divine moment of positive change.

Do not judge others, and you will not be judged. For you will be treated as you treat others. The standard you use in judging is the standard by which you will be judged. And why worry about a speck in your friend's eye when you have a log in your own? MATTHEW 7:1-3

☼ **A prayer for GENTLENESS**
When I underestimate the power of gentleness

DEAR JESUS,

When the Bible tells me to pursue gentleness, I know it does not mean that I am to be a doormat and let others walk all over me. In fact, you are the perfect example of gentleness, and yet you are also a mighty warrior who defeated the powers of hell. When I am tempted to exert power over others inappropriately, help me to respond with gentleness instead, that I might accomplish your will.

Since God chose you to be the holy people he loves, you must clothe yourselves with tenderhearted mercy, kindness, humility, gentleness, and patience. COLOSSIANS 3:12

DAY 161 *Prayerful Moment*

☼ **A prayer for HURTS**
When I've been hurt by someone

GOD,

Thank you that when you forgive, you wipe away the past and forget it. You forgive perfectly, but when I am dealing with people who have hurt me, I find forgiveness difficult. I know I can't control their actions; I can only choose whether to forgive. Help me to follow your example so that I don't end up with a bitter spirit. Only by forgiving others will I be free to experience your forgiveness.

If you forgive those who sin against you, your heavenly Father will forgive you. MATTHEW 6:14

⚙ **A prayer for CREATIVITY**
When I need a little inspiration

GOD,

Creativity is the overflow of a full heart and mind. But sometimes I feel empty. Other times I feel as if my mind is full of the wrong material. How can I fill myself with the kind of beauty that spills out in meaningful ideas, sounds, words, and movements? By taking the time to focus on what is beautiful and what is true. If creativity can be an expression of your beauty, God, then I must always fill up on your Spirit and wisdom. I commit to take time to know you and to soak up what is beautiful. Thank you, God, that when I think about all your creative works in the world around me, your Spirit inspires my heart and mind so that creativity can flow out of my life in productive ways.

Fix your thoughts on what is true, and honorable, and right, and pure, and lovely, and admirable. Think about things that are excellent and worthy of praise. Keep putting into practice all you learned and received from me—everything you heard from me and saw me doing. Then the God of peace will be with you. PHILIPPIANS 4:8-9

☀ **A prayer for DIGNITY**
When I need a better definition of dignity

ALMIGHTY GOD,

Every human being has been given dignity because we are created in your image. If that's true, why don't I act like it? So often I fail to acknowledge that worth in myself and others. I tend to rank everyone from important to insignificant. In my own mind, I always come out as superior, of course. No, that is not dignity. Oh, that you would open my eyes to see others as you see them, worthy of my love and respect. Help me to claim the dignity you have given to me. May I act respectably, with self-control, strong faith, love, and patience. Instead of ranking others beneath me, let me build them up to be served above me. And help me to realize how you esteem me, Lord, so that I may be at peace with my own worth and the worth of others.

You made [people] only a little lower than God and crowned them with glory and honor. PSALM 8:5

☀ **A prayer for FREEDOM**
When I feel trapped by my own sinful desires

DEAR GOD,

I used to think that freedom meant I could do anything or have anything I wanted. That just made me a slave to my own desires. Soon I found myself trapped in destructive habits, hurtful relationships, and even powerful addictions. That is not freedom. That's bondage. When I learned about Jesus, I saw the truth: I am a needy person who needs a merciful God. Only you can provide what I am looking for. Only you can provide the path to freedom. Thank you for teaching me that freedom is found in living a life consistent with truth, in a way that keeps my heart, mind, body, and soul all free. True freedom comes when the reality of your holiness overpowers my sinful inclinations and fills my life with the fullness of your liberating love.

The Scriptures declare that we are all prisoners of sin, so we receive God's promise of freedom only by believing in Jesus Christ. GALATIANS 3:22

☀ **A prayer for HOLINESS**
When I long to be more holy before God

LORD OF HEAVEN AND EARTH,
My desire is to be holy. To be holy is to be sinless, pure, and perfect before you. I cannot accomplish that in my present body, but I can work toward that goal until I reach my final destination. Someday I will stand before you, cleansed and forgiven, in heaven. But for now, I can try to renounce sin each day. Part of holiness means to be set apart, different—to live as you want me to live and not how the world assumes I should live. May I long for your smile more than the world's approval. Please bless my desire to be holy on my earthly journey. May I one day arrive at my final destination and stand, redeemed and completely holy, before you.

I plead with you to give your bodies to God because of all he has done for you. Let them be a living and holy sacrifice—the kind he will find acceptable. ROMANS 12:1

⚙ **A prayer about NEEDS**
When I feel discontented despite having all I need

DEAR JESUS,

I feel guilty for feeling discontented, because I have all that I need. I confess that I spend so much energy thinking about what I want and plotting how to get it. I know this is wrong, and I experience such anxiety because of this habit. I'd rather live contentedly in obedience to you than spend my whole life fussing over things. Help me to recognize the difference between things I need and things I want. I pray that my needs would be opportunities for you to show your power and provision and to teach me that you are sufficient. Help me depend on you so that I can find contentment as I see you meet my needs. Please lead my heart to desire the same things that you do.

Don't love money; be satisfied with what you have. For God has said, "I will never fail you. I will never abandon you."
HEBREWS 13:5

☼ **A prayer about the SUPERNATURAL**
   Can I experience the supernatural?

DEAR GOD,

The presence of your Holy Spirit within me is evidence of the supernatural. Your Spirit teaches me and reveals to me things I cannot see with my natural eyes. He gives me the insight to recognize your hand at work and empowers me to love others even when they oppose you. Through your Spirit, I can find overwhelming peace in the midst of great suffering, and think of others before myself. Thank you for the gift of your Spirit in my life.

We have received God's Spirit (not the world's spirit), so we can know the wonderful things God has freely given us.
1 CORINTHIANS 2:12

DAY 168 *Prayerful Moment*

☼ **A prayer of COMPASSION**
   When I want to reflect Christ's compassion in ways that touch others

PRECIOUS JESUS,

There are times when I'm not moved by the incredible pain around me, either because I am too self-focused or because my heart is unresponsive to you. Please don't let my heart become hardened. Fill me with your compassion and love for those who are hurting or in need.

The LORD is good to everyone. He showers compassion on all his creation. PSALM 145:9

⚙ **A prayer of PRAISE**
*When I enter God's presence and think on all
he has done*

HOLY GOD,

Praise is creation's natural response to your greatness. It is not unusual for people to burst into spontaneous applause when a head of state or a celebrity enters a room. And when I enter your presence through worship, my natural response should be praise. The Bible teaches that you created the universe. That you hold all of creation in your hands and yet care deeply for the details of my life is amazing. Truly you alone are worthy of my highest praise. When I consider who you are and what you have done for me, praise is the only possible response! Jesus said that if people didn't lift their voices to worship, the very rocks and stones would cry out in praise to you. I lift my voice to you now and glorify you. I admire you, respect you, and long to give you glory my whole life long.

Great is the LORD! He is most worthy of praise! He is to be feared above all gods. The gods of other nations are mere idols, but the LORD made the heavens!
I CHRONICLES 16:25-26

⚙ **A prayer in SORROW**
When I'm in deep distress

HEAVENLY FATHER,

I am going through my own Valley of Weeping. Like everyone's, my life has included many times of struggle and tears. Tragic losses affect me profoundly. Your Word acknowledges that sorrow and grief are part of human life, and faith in you does not keep me from going through difficult times. Rather, my faith enables me to walk through those times and grow stronger along the way. I take heart in the knowledge that sorrow does not have the last word. I have great hope in your promise to redeem my losses in heaven. In your promises of eternal life, I find the hope and comfort to carry me through life's valleys.

What joy for those whose strength comes from the LORD, who have set their minds on a pilgrimage to Jerusalem. When they walk through the Valley of Weeping, it will become a place of refreshing springs. The autumn rains will clothe it with blessings. They will continue to grow stronger, and each of them will appear before God in Jerusalem.
PSALM 84:5-7

☼ **A prayer about REWARDS**
When there seems to be no reward for following God

GOD,

I like results. I usually choose my activities based on what will bring the maximum reward and the greatest sense of accomplishment. This is why I struggle sometimes to obey you. I know that you reward obedience, because your Word gives me examples such as Caleb, who inherited the Promised Land, and the widow Ruth, who was given a husband. But these were physical blessings. I struggle to obey when I know the rewards aren't material. For example, I know that my obedience to you often protects me from unseen evil and allows you to lead me along paths of righteousness into service that pleases you and helps others. Those are wonderful reasons to obey you, so why do I see them as less important than the things that bring me immediate, tangible rewards? Lord, help me to let go of my desire for material blessings or earthly prosperity. Give me a desire for spiritual rewards—the marvelous gifts of salvation and eternal life, the blessings of your presence in my life, the treasure of your Word, and the wonderful character traits of godliness, integrity, wisdom, hope, peace, love, and a good reputation. These rewards are eternal and priceless.

Don't store up treasures here on earth, where moths eat them and rust destroys them, and where thieves break in and steal. Store your treasures in heaven, where moths and rust cannot destroy, and thieves do not break in and steal.
MATTHEW 6:19-20

☼ A prayer about TEMPTATION
When I need to arm myself against temptation

DEAR JESUS,

Satan has the power to overwhelm me if it's just me against him. But with you, Jesus, Satan has no power. When you live in me in the form of the Holy Spirit, your power becomes available to me, and then Satan can be overwhelmed. Because of the Holy Spirit, I have the advantage in overcoming any temptation. The devil can tempt me, but he cannot coerce me. He can dangle the bait in front of me, but he cannot force me to take it. He'll try every trick in the book to make me think I'm missing out, that I cannot and should not resist. But I can break free from temptation when I change my focus from what's in front of me to who is inside me. Then I can discern the difference between the lies of temptation and the truth of your Word, between what seems so right and what's really right. Dear Jesus, please help me think not about what I'm missing, but about what I'll be gaining by obeying you and resisting temptation. Thank you that I have far more power available to me than I realize. When I arm myself with your Word and rely on the presence of your Spirit within me, temptations become moments in which I can experience your power helping me overcome.

Every child of God defeats this evil world, and we achieve this victory through our faith. And who can win this battle against the world? Only those who believe that Jesus is the Son of God. 1 JOHN 5:4-5

☼ **A prayer about CONFORMITY**
*When I've been doing what's popular rather than
what is godly*

DEAR GOD,

The society I live in imposes its shape on me. It tries to
mold me into its way of looking, thinking, and behaving. The mold is strong, and at times I have even lived in
fear of breaking it. But that approach has consequences.
I realize now that my life has not taken the shape you
intended for me. Unfortunately, culture rarely values your
standards. Many people say, "I'm going to do what I want.
I don't care what people say." But I believe in you, God. I
know that my task is to conform to your way of thinking
and acting, even when it goes against what's popular. I
have a special responsibility to act as your representative. If
my actions are not consistent with my faith, I could cause
others to question your life-changing power to mold me
into your masterpiece. My conformity to your ways reveals
my freedom from cultural influence. May my behavior
cause others to ask about my faith as they see me living
out your ways. Reshape me into your image, and cause my
life to take on the form you intended for me.

*O LORD, you are our Father. We are the clay, and you are
the potter. We all are formed by your hand.* ISAIAH 64:8

☼ **A prayer for LOVE**
Am I prepared to sacrifice for those I love?

FATHER GOD,

Jesus said that there is no greater love than to give up my life for a friend. Though I may never have to physically die on a friend's behalf, Jesus' words prompt a poignant question: What am I willing to sacrifice to show his love to someone? Father, what can I do today to "lay down my life" to show the love of Jesus to a friend or a neighbor?

[Jesus said,] "This is my commandment: Love each other in the same way I have loved you. There is no greater love than to lay down one's life for one's friends." JOHN 15:12-13

DAY 175 *Prayerful Moment*

☼ **A prayer about STRENGTH**
When I'm tempted to trust in my own power

ALMIGHTY GOD,

I have learned that my abilities do not always make me strong. In fact, the demands of life often reveal my weakness. But your wisdom and power are frequently demonstrated through human weakness. When I try to depend on my own strength, I close myself off to your infinite power. Work through me, Lord, in ways that would be impossible in my own strength.

I am glad to boast about my weaknesses, so that the power of Christ can work through me. 2 CORINTHIANS 12:9

DAY 176

⚙ **A prayer about WITNESSING**
  When I'm afraid to speak about my faith

DEAR JESUS,

When I hear the term "witness," I am immediately turned off. My first image is of pushy evangelists knocking on people's doors. But to witness simply means to tell about something I have experienced. Your Word says that all who believe in you share the privilege and responsibility of being witnesses, or simply sharing what we've experienced with you. Believing in you isn't about getting in some exclusive group. It's about experiencing something so wonderful that I can't wait to invite others to find it too. Lord Jesus, I have been so afraid of sharing about you that I feel unprepared. When the right time arises, help me to be ready to tell the story of how I met and grew to love you. That is the greatest story I can tell. May my own story be the pathway to a divine moment in another's life.

God has not given us a spirit of fear and timidity, but of power, love, and self-discipline. So never be ashamed to tell others about our Lord. 2 TIMOTHY 1:7-8

☀ **A prayer for a clear CONSCIENCE**
When I need God to examine my motives

O GOD,

I know my motives are often less than pure. Too many of my decisions are made with only me in mind. Jesus taught that our words flow from what's in our heart. So when my motives are selfish or impure, it is only a matter of time before my words and actions also become selfish and impure. Because the condition of my heart is the key, that's what you are most concerned about. Father God, you alone know my heart. I may be able to fool others and even myself at times, but I can't fool you. Holy Father, I welcome your examination of my heart and my motives. Shine the light of your Spirit into the dark corners of my heart, so that I will be able to act with a clear conscience. Then my heart will be more prepared for you to do a great work in me and through me.

May the words of my mouth and the meditation of my heart be pleasing to you, O LORD, my rock and my redeemer. PSALM 19:14

☼ A prayer about OPPOSITION
*When I seem to encounter opposition as I'm trying to
do what God wants*

LORD OF HEAVEN'S ARMIES,

As I stay faithful to you, I know I can expect persistent
opposition from those who don't want to see your work
succeed. Those who oppose you will never stop trying to
oppose the work your people do for you. Spiritual adversaries won't quit after one or two attempts to defeat me.
This kind of opposition will be a lifetime struggle because
it is a spiritual battle against the forces of darkness. O
Lord, where will I find the strength to endure? When I
encounter resistance, I begin to experience frustration and
despair. O Lord, my hope is in you! You promise to supply
me with all the strength I need. May I prepare carefully for
the extended conflict ahead. Please give me patient determination and confident hope that victory belongs to you!
When I face opposition, may I rejoice that I am living
effectively enough for you that your enemies are taking
notice. Then I can look at each battle as an opportunity to
experience a divine moment of victory.

*If you are suffering in a manner that pleases God, keep on
doing what is right, and trust your lives to the God who
created you, for he will never fail you.* I PETER 4:19

☀ A prayer for PREPARATION
When I want to be prepared for a life of spiritual adventure

FATHER,

This is a prayer of preparation, because I want to be ready for whatever you have in store for me. First, please prepare me to make wise decisions at a moment's notice. Help me to develop wisdom over time so that when a difficult situation comes, I will have accumulated the spiritual depth to know the right thing to do. May I be ready to act swiftly and decisively because I have a wellspring of wisdom to draw upon. Second, please prepare me for temptation so that when I meet it face-to-face, I will recognize it and know how to combat it. Train me in quiet times so I will have the spiritual wisdom, strength, and commitment to honor you in the face of intense desires and testing. Third, please prepare me for worship by showing me how to get my heart right with you. Fourth, please prepare me to explain my faith and why it is important. Teach me the great truths from your Word. And finally, please prepare me to defend my faith. When attacks come, may I have already developed the skill to hear the Holy Spirit, who will help me speak with authority and courage. Please prepare me, Lord, so I can be all you want me to be for your service.

Be strong in the Lord and in his mighty power. Put on all of God's armor so that you will be able to stand firm against all strategies of the devil. EPHESIANS 6:10-11

☼ A prayer about CONSCIENCE
When I need to sharpen my conscience

DEAR LORD GOD,

Thank you for my conscience, which is your gift to keep me sensitive to your moral code for living. My conscience helps me understand when I have fallen out of line with your will. But I must use this gift to keep it sharp. Help me always to listen to and obey my conscience, for if I don't, it will become harder and harder to hear. I can't afford for it to malfunction and lead me astray, convincing me that right is wrong and wrong is right. May I keep my conscience finely tuned by staying close to you, spending time in your Word, and making an effort to understand my own tendencies toward right and wrong. May it always provide me with a strong inner sense of accountability about what is true and right. If I am increasingly unmoved by evil or injustice, remind me that my conscience is becoming dulled. O Lord, please continue to sharpen my conscience so that I consistently speak in harmony with your Word.

Cling to your faith in Christ, and keep your conscience clear.
For some people have deliberately violated their consciences;
as a result, their faith has been shipwrecked.

I TIMOTHY I:19

☼ A prayer about MISTAKES
*When I wonder if God can use me despite
my mistakes*

MERCIFUL GOD,

How amazing that you can redeem my mistakes. I never want to take that for granted or use it as an excuse to sin. Still, the wonder of grace is that you can use my worst failures to strengthen my faith and enable me to better comfort and help others. Thank you, Lord.

The LORD directs the steps of the godly. He delights in every detail of their lives. Though they stumble, they will never fall, for the LORD holds them by the hand. PSALM 37:23-24

DAY 182 *Prayerful Moment*

☼ A prayer about CONSEQUENCES
When I am suffering the consequences of my actions

O GOD,

Forgive me for using the sharpness of my tongue to hurt my friend. It's too late to undo the consequences. I cannot retract my words; they've done their damage. But now I have a choice to humble myself and ask my friend for forgiveness. Lord, I pray that you will redeem my foolishness and bring something positive from this situation.

Plant the good seeds of righteousness, and you will harvest a crop of love. Plow up the hard ground of your hearts, for now is the time to seek the LORD, that he may come and shower righteousness upon you. HOSEA 10:12

☼ A prayer for CONVICTION
When I'm seeking conviction to strengthen my faith

DEAR LORD,

There are two kinds of conviction I ask from you. First, I need the conviction of knowing what is true and right. Please help me to know truth, to rightly discern what your Word says. Second, I need your Holy Spirit to teach my heart so that I can know how to live out these truths effectively. It isn't enough to know what to believe. I must live out those beliefs in a way that draws me closer to you and sets a good example for others who are growing in their faith. Thank you for the Holy Spirit, who convicts my heart. Please keep my convictions firm, that my life might be an accurate picture of your grace, truth, and love.

[The responsibility of church leaders] will continue until we all come to such unity in our faith and knowledge of God's Son that we will be mature in the Lord, measuring up to the full and complete standard of Christ. Then we will no longer be immature like children. We won't be tossed and blown about by every wind of new teaching. We will not be influenced when people try to trick us with lies so clever they sound like the truth. Instead, we will speak the truth in love, growing in every way more and more like Christ, who is the head of his body, the church. EPHESIANS 4:13-15

DAY 184

☼ A prayer of ENCOURAGEMENT
Letting God's encouragement renew my life

DEAR GOD,

Joshua was a great leader who succeeded Moses. But his resolve may have weakened as he took over the daunting task of leading the Israelites into a land of giants. So you prepared him—and the rest of the people—with specific words of encouragement. Sometimes I long for someone to come beside me to encourage and strengthen me. How much better if that someone is you! O God, your encouragement helps me to press on, to renew my commitment and resolve. It inspires me with the hope that my task is not in vain, that I can make a difference. Your encouragement is a beautiful gift—a spiritual gift that gives me a renewed desire and commitment to obey you. I will find encouragement not by looking within or around me but by looking up to you, my Sovereign God.

Be strong and courageous! Do not be afraid or discouraged. For the LORD your God is with you wherever you go.
JOSHUA 1:9

⚙ **A prayer about EVIL**
When I want to distance myself from evil

ALMIGHTY GOD,

How I praise you that ultimately you will judge all evil at the last day. But there have also been times here on earth when your anger against evil was poured out in judgment. You rose up and said, "Enough!" People who live an evil lifestyle put themselves in harm's way enough times that harm eventually comes to them. O God, help me not to get so close to evil that I find myself in harm's way because of your righteous and imminent judgment. Please fill me with your Spirit so that I am not attracted to those who do evil. Don't let me become like them. May I never be so in touch with evil that it suddenly dawns on me just how dangerous my situation is. Grant me the grace to be strengthened by those who love you and wholeheartedly follow you.

The LORD watches over the path of the godly, but the path of the wicked leads to destruction. PSALM 1:6

☼ A prayer about DEMANDS
When life's demands seem impossible

ALMIGHTY GOD,

I am going through a time in my life when the demands on me seem impossible. The task is too hard, the burden too much to bear, and my schedule too full to keep up with. Sometimes only my faith keeps me going because I know my greatest source of help is you, almighty God. You are God of the impossible. When life's demands pile up, my only option is to turn to you. I acknowledge my need for help beyond what human hands can supply. I give control of my life to you and ask you to carry the burden for me. I need you to give me the strength to continue.

He gives power to the weak and strength to the powerless. Even youths will become weak and tired, and young men will fall in exhaustion. But those who trust in the LORD will find new strength. They will soar high on wings like eagles. They will run and not grow weary. They will walk and not faint. ISAIAH 40:29-31

☼ **A prayer for COURAGE**
When I need to face my greatest fears

MY LORD AND MY GOD,

Over the centuries your church has been constantly threatened with persecution. Those strong in their faith did not pray for the threats to be taken away but for the courage to face them. I know that you are powerful enough to take away the things that frighten me. But I also know that more often you would rather give me the boldness to turn my fears into opportunities for spiritual growth and for helping others. Oh, how I wish you would take away my troubles. But when you don't, grant me the courage to face them head-on and the confidence to know that when you help me through them, I will be a mightier spiritual warrior, better equipped to live boldly for you. After all, if you took away everything that frightened me, there would be no need for hope. And it is hope that helps me see beyond my immediate crisis and place my current fears, as well as my eternal future, in your hands. My hope is not in protecting myself, but in becoming more like you. Yes, Lord, may I desire courage more than comfort.

Having hope will give you courage. JOB 11:18

☼ **A prayer about STRESS**
When I am feeling intense levels of stress

LORD GOD,

I ask for the gift of your eternal perspective. I confess that I have allowed the cares of this world to cloud my mind and steal the joy from my heart. But what are the troubles of today compared to the gift of your salvation? Lord, I know with your help I can rise above the simple cares of this world. Give me the peace that only you can give.

I have told you all this so that you may have peace in me. Here on earth you will have many trials and sorrows. But take heart, because I have overcome the world. JOHN 16:33

DAY 189 *Prayerful Moment*

☼ **A prayer about QUITTING**
When I feel like quitting

DEAR GOD,

I think of *quitting* as a bad word, but I know there are times when I should quit—such as when I am doing something wrong, or if I am hurting someone else. However, may I never quit a task that you have called me to do, no matter how hard it seems. Give me the strength to persevere when the going gets tough. Help me to keep my eyes fixed on you as I move forward boldly in faith.

Let's not get tired of doing what is good. At just the right time we will reap a harvest of blessing if we don't give up. GALATIANS 6:9

☼ A prayer about IMAGINATION
Is using my imagination okay?

HOLY GOD,

You are the epitome of creativity, and I am made in your image! If you were able to imagine the heavens and earth and animals and humans, and I am patterned after you, then you have certainly instilled some imaginative abilities in me. Since you are the ultimate creator, you are the source of my creative abilities. Some people use their imaginations to design skyscrapers, paint a beautiful picture, write music, or revolutionize the way others think about you. I pray that in whatever way I use my imagination, the result would always be honorable and pleasing to you. Let my creative abilities express my gratitude to you for making me in your image.

Moses told the people of Israel, "The LORD has specifically chosen Bezalel. . . . The LORD has filled Bezalel with the Spirit of God, giving him great wisdom, ability, and expertise in all kinds of crafts." EXODUS 35:30-31

☀ A prayer of HONESTY
When I feel like taking shortcuts

LORD,

I know that my honesty matters to you because it reveals my character. If I'm in the habit of cheating in little things, I'll have a hard time being honest when bigger challenges with bigger stakes come my way. It doesn't matter if no one else is watching—God, you are. Even if no one else knows, you know. You see my true character, which is revealed in those moments when I think no one is looking. If my honesty can't be trusted in a small matter, it can't be trusted in a big matter. Lord, I want to build my life with the bricks of honesty so I will have a strong foundation of integrity when challenges come my way. Let my life be governed by your standards of fairness and justice. May I be trustworthy even in the small things.

Who may climb the mountain of the LORD? Who may stand in his holy place? Only those whose hands and hearts are pure, who do not worship idols and never tell lies. They will receive the LORD's blessing and have a right relationship with God their savior. PSALM 24:3-5

☼ A prayer for EXCELLENCE
Why it is important to strive for excellence

DEAR GOD,

I want to be a person of excellence—one who exceeds others' expectations—for that is a rare thing in this world. Yes, I want to strive for excellence in a life skill, just like a medical doctor trying to exceed expectations might develop a new vaccine that saves people's lives. But most of all I want to be excellent in the way I live as one of your followers. Please allow me to care deeply about telling the truth, about doing things well and right, about helping those in need. May my pursuit of excellent character give others a glimpse of your character. May my striving inspire them to pursue a purpose beyond themselves. You initiated excellence in the beauty of your creation, and we are called to perpetuate it. I know I display excellence when I consistently model myself after Jesus Christ, who is perfect. Since I will never be perfect in this life, there is always something to strive for!

Work willingly at whatever you do, as though you were working for the Lord rather than for people. Remember that the Lord will give you an inheritance as your reward, and that the Master you are serving is Christ.

COLOSSIANS 3:23-24

☼ **A prayer about WORK**
When the work I do seems meaningless

DEAR GOD,

Work is anchored in your character, and part of being made in your image is sharing the industrious and creative aspects of your nature. You are a God of excellence and commitment, and I long to exhibit those same qualities, especially at work. Some days my job is great, and other days I feel unmotivated or stressed. But I know that whatever task I am called upon to do, I have an opportunity to demonstrate a divine standard of excellence and commitment, both to my assignments and to those around me. Lord, please teach me to work diligently and with enthusiasm at whatever I do, whether I'm on the job or at home with my family. When I think of my daily tasks as having been assigned by you, I find myself working for your approval, and I am often proud of the work I do. But more important, God, I want you to be proud of me. I'm so thankful that I have an opportunity to show creativity and responsibility in each task of my day. Please help my efforts be an inspiration for others to glorify you in all they do each day.

My life is worth nothing to me unless I use it for finishing the work assigned me by the Lord Jesus—the work of telling others the Good News about the wonderful grace of God. ACTS 20:24

DAY 194

☼ A prayer of ACCEPTANCE
When it's hard to accept others

DEAR GOD,

You accept me no matter what—despite the times I've hurt you, ignored you, or rejected you. You call me to accept others the same way you do. Just as you first accept me wherever I am in life and *then* challenge me to change and grow, so I must accept others before I try to influence them. Help me to remember that acceptance isn't about befriending the best or most godly people. Rather, acceptance is about letting you break through my fears, inhibitions, and stereotypes to bring out the best in the people around me. God, empower me also to respond to your call to accept those the world deems unacceptable— the poor, the homeless, the handicapped, the elderly, prisoners, and addicts. Please work through me, Lord.

Accept each other just as Christ has accepted you so that God will be given glory. ROMANS 15:7

☀ A prayer for MEANING
When I'm looking for more meaning in this life

DEAR GOD OVER ALL THINGS,

As a heaven-bound follower of yours, help me always to put heaven and earth in proper perspective. As I focus on the unique role you have planned for me in eternity, help me to find purpose and meaning in how I live each day until then. May my thoughts, plans, words, and actions be an investment in my eternal future.

Our present troubles are small and won't last very long. Yet they produce for us a glory that vastly outweighs them and will last forever! 2 CORINTHIANS 4:17

☀ A prayer for COURAGE
When I'm feeling alone and afraid

LORD GOD,

Sometimes the challenges of life make me fearful. Help me to remember that you are stronger than my biggest problem or my worst enemy. Thank you for helping me with your limitless power. I know that courage doesn't come from confidence in my own strength, but only from confidence in you. Thank you for the courage to face whatever lies ahead.

Don't be afraid, for I am with you. Don't be discouraged, for I am your God. I will strengthen you and help you. I will hold you up with my victorious right hand. ISAIAH 41:10

☀ **A prayer when in DOUBT**
When I wonder if my doubts mean I have less faith

DEAR GOD OF THE UNIVERSE,

I'm struggling with doubt, and that worries me. Is my faith ebbing? As I read your Word, though, it strikes me how many "pillars of the faith" had moments of great doubt. In most cases they didn't have less faith at those moments, but instead their faith was being challenged in new ways. As I face my own doubts, I wonder if that is what is happening to me. Maybe my moments of doubt aren't shaking my faith but challenging it to grow stronger. Doubts put me in new territory, where life is uncertain and unknown. But my uncertainty in one area shouldn't cause me to reject what I know for sure in another area. So, Lord, because of my certainty in who you are—the loving and gracious God of all things—please use my doubts to move me closer to you, not further away.

Jesus told [Thomas], "You believe because you have seen me. Blessed are those who believe without seeing me."
JOHN 20:29

☀ A prayer about ADDICTION
When I struggle with addiction or bad habits

DEAR JESUS,

I admit that I am struggling with addictive behaviors. In the moment of temptation, I can easily justify giving in just this once, thinking I have things under control. But I realize that my "one time" has turned into a habit I can't stop. It now controls me. Ironically, the only way to recover my self-control is to let you control me. Jesus, your control is always for my benefit and for my spiritual growth. When I give you control of my life, you can break the power of any addiction I am struggling with. Thank you! Jesus, I realize that to overcome addiction, I need the consistent support of people who love me enough to hold me accountable. But I also want to hold myself accountable to your way of living. This will keep me close to you so you can work in my life to change my heart and desires. I surrender to your Holy Spirit, and ask you to replace my addictive impulses with life-affirming desires. While it is important that I seek the help of others, it is only with *your* help that I will ultimately have the power to overcome.

The Holy Spirit produces this kind of fruit in our lives: love, joy, peace, patience, kindness, goodness, faithfulness, gentleness, and self-control. GALATIANS 5:22-23

☀ A prayer for DELIVERANCE
Jesus delivers me from sin

DEAR JESUS,

I praise you that you came to deliver people who are oppressed by the world or the powers of evil. I see this in the Gospel accounts of you delivering people from spiritual oppression by demons. You delivered some from physical oppression by healing their diseases. You delivered others from intellectual oppression by exposing lies and teaching the truth that sets us free. And you spoke boldly against the injustice of abusive leadership, especially against religious leaders. I see now why salvation is also called deliverance. Jesus, I believe that you can deliver me not only from the consequences of my sins but also from the forces in this world that oppress me. Be my deliverer, Jesus.

[Jesus said,] "The Spirit of the LORD is upon me, for he has anointed me to bring Good News to the poor. He has sent me to proclaim that captives will be released, that the blind will see, that the oppressed will be set free, and that the time of the LORD's favor has come." LUKE 4:18-19

DAY 200

⚙ **A prayer about PRAYER**
*Trusting God through prayer helps me accept
his answers*

HEAVENLY FATHER,

Thank you that you listen carefully to every prayer and
answer me. You are my heavenly Father, and I know that
you love me and want what is best for me. Therefore, I
know I can trust you whether you answer my prayers with
a *yes*, *no*, or even *wait*. Doesn't any loving parent give all
three of these responses to a child? I'm glad you do not
spoil me by giving in to my every whim. How often have
I asked you for things that later I realized were not pleasing to you? But you do not always answer no. You are
not a vindictive, stingy God. You love to give abundantly
to your children because you are generous and merciful.
While I often am frustrated when you ask me to wait, I
know that you don't just put my requests on hold because
you're too busy to respond. Instead, your answer is often
delayed to make me ready or to open my eyes to what is
best for me. Father, I rejoice in talking with you because I
know you will answer in a way that is perfect and wise.

*I love the LORD because he hears my voice and my prayer for
mercy.* PSALM 116:1

⚙ **A prayer of ASSURANCE**
  When the certainty of heaven brings hope to this life

HEAVENLY FATHER,

Your promises about heaven are as certain as all of your other promises. I believe that when I've entrusted my life to you, you will certainly guard my eternal future because of your deep love for me. Ultimately, God, it is your hold on me, not my grip on you, that matters most. I am saved by faith in you, not by my own efforts. Because of your steadfast hold on me, I can be strong and courageous as I seek to follow where you lead in this life. And I can be confident that your promise of eternal life and the future you have planned for me is far better than I can ever imagine! Lord, I ask for the faith to be able to live as if I believe that today.

For God loved the world so much that he gave his one and only Son, so that everyone who believes in him will not perish but have eternal life. JOHN 3:16

☼ A prayer about FUN
When I enjoy the blessings God has given me

DEAR GOD,

Judging from the number of feasts and festivals you decreed for the Israelites, it seems you intended for your people to have fun. You want us to laugh and enjoy life, because this gives us a taste of the joy we will experience in heaven. Thank you for lifting my spirits and opening my heart to joy and laughter. And thank you for blessing me with a taste of eternity.

He fills my life with good things. PSALM 103:5

DAY 203 *Prayerful Moment*

☼ A prayer for the HEART
When I need to guard my heart

O LORD,

I know that whatever I do springs from the condition of my heart. An act of kindness doesn't come from an evil heart, and generosity doesn't spring from a stingy heart. Please stand guard at the door of my heart. Don't allow wrong thoughts and desires to sneak in and set up house. I know I can't trust myself to keep my heart clean, but I can trust your Word, because it comes from your heart, which is good and perfect.

Guard your heart above all else, for it determines the course of your life. PROVERBS 4:23

☀ A prayer for EMPATHY
When I want be in tune with others

O LORD,

I try to understand others, but sometimes I lack the empathy to connect with them and feel their joy or pain. I need you to teach me empathy. I know I lack it because I sometimes feel jealousy over a friend's success or find myself enjoying the failure of an enemy. That doesn't reflect your heart. If I were able to genuinely feel what another person feels—to experience the very same emotions he or she experiences—there would be no room for jealousy or competition. O Lord, as you teach me empathy, break through to my own heart, softening it toward others and helping me know how to comfort them, support them, and meet their needs. I'm tired of acting sad for hurting people or pretending to be happy for the joys of others. No, I want to be genuinely sorrowful with those who hurt and genuinely joyful with the successes of others. May I learn empathy so I can be responsive to the needs of others!

Be happy with those who are happy, and weep with those who weep. ROMANS 12:15

DAY 205

⚙ **A prayer of SURPRISE**
Realizing that God isn't defined by my expectations

DEAR GOD,

You never cease to amaze me. You often do the opposite of what I would expect. You chose David, the youngest son of Jesse, to be king of Israel instead of his tall, strong, oldest brother. You took Saul, the most vicious opponent of the early church, and transformed him into Paul, the greatest and most courageous missionary of all time. You cared for and respected women in a time when they had no rights. And you used a crucifixion, the ultimate defeat, and made it the sign of victory over sin and death for all eternity. Your creativity and ingenuity know no boundaries. How often do I miss something wonderful you've done because I am expecting something else? God, don't let me limit you to my own understanding, but allow me to recognize you in ways that inspire awe, love, gratitude, and joy.

Come and see what our God has done, what awesome miracles he performs for people! PSALM 66:5

☼ **A prayer about EMOTION**
   When I want to express my emotions in a godly way

MY GOD AND MY CREATOR,

How amazing that you would gift me with emotions! They are evidence that I am made in your image, for the Bible shows you displaying the whole range of emotions from anger to zeal. My feelings allow me to drink deeply of the wonderful blessings you have given me, to feel sorrow over sin, and to empathize with others who need comfort. But they can also be easily hijacked by my wayward heart. So often I'm caught in a tug-of-war between my sinful desires and my desire for holiness. When my desires oppose one another, the same emotion can have two outlets—one good and the other bad. Lord, you created emotions, so you can teach me how to reclaim my feelings to be used for righteous ends. Please help me to control my desires and to channel my emotions into holy expressions.

When you follow the desires of your sinful nature, the results are very clear: sexual immorality, impurity, lustful pleasures, idolatry, sorcery, hostility, quarreling, jealousy, outbursts of anger, selfish ambition, dissension, division, envy, drunkenness, wild parties, and other sins like these. Let me tell you again, as I have before, that anyone living that sort of life will not inherit the Kingdom of God. But the Holy Spirit produces this kind of fruit in our lives: love, joy, peace, patience, kindness, goodness, faithfulness, gentleness, and self-control. There is no law against these things! GALATIANS 5:19-23

⚙ **A prayer about EMPTINESS**
When I need God to fill the emptiness inside me

O LORD,

I'm on empty. I've lost motivation, meaning, and purpose, and my life no longer satisfies. How can my empty heart be filled? I know Satan is ready to move right into my empty heart and make himself at home. He wants to deceive me into thinking that what he offers can satisfy me and refill my empty tank. But God, only you can fill the emptiness inside me and satisfy my deepest needs. Please refill my heart. Refill me with the pure love, truth, and goodness that only come from you. Fill my heart so full that evil has no room to enter. For it is only through the presence of your Holy Spirit within me that meaning, purpose, and satisfaction will be restored. May my soul once again be fulfilled. My heart has opened to you, and I am ready.

I pray that God, the source of hope, will fill you completely with joy and peace because you trust in him. Then you will overflow with confident hope through the power of the Holy Spirit. ROMANS 15:13

☼ A prayer about PERSECUTION
When I'm harassed for my faith in Jesus

DEAR JESUS,

I have hung on to my faith in you, and you have blessed me because of it. As I've endured testing, my faith has become strong and genuine. Sometimes the hardest tests have been times when I was scorned, mocked, or ignored by others because of my trust in you. During these hard times, my character was revealed and forced to grow. Persecution has a way of showing a person's true colors and making known his or her level of commitment to you. As I've endured hardships, I've found that my faith is real. I praise you for that! Your Word encourages me with stories about many people who never stopped trusting you even though they were mocked, persecuted, and even killed for their faith. I may never face martyrdom for being a Christian, but I pray that my faith is strong enough to endure persecution like that. Let me live boldly for you, despite opposition, so I might make a great impact for eternity.

The more we suffer for Christ, the more God will shower us with his comfort through Christ. 2 CORINTHIANS 1:5

☼ A prayer about ADAPTABILITY
When I need stability amid life's changes

DEAR JESUS,

My ability to adapt to life's changes goes hand in hand with trusting you. When the road of life takes a sudden sharp turn, I can adapt willingly and quickly because I know that you love me, and I trust that you have the best plans for my life. Thus I'm able to move forward in faith and obedience to you.

I am the LORD, and I do not change. MALACHI 3:6

DAY 210 *Prayerful Moment*

☼ A prayer about FEAR
When I need God's strength to help me with my fears

STRONG AND MIGHTY SAVIOR,

There are no limits to what you can do in and through me. With your strength, I have the power to do things I could never do on my own. I can withstand the toughest attacks and overcome my problems. I can live without fear because I will rely on your strength. Please show me how to give all of my fears to you, Jesus, so I can live through your power and not my own.

I love you, LORD; you are my strength. The LORD is my rock, my fortress, and my savior; my God is my rock, in whom I find protection. He is my shield, the power that saves me, and my place of safety. . . . In your strength I can crush an army; with my God I can scale any wall. PSALM 18:1-2, 29

☼ A prayer for PATIENCE
When I become anxious or annoyed easily

JESUS,

Forgive me. I have been more frustrated than usual. I long for your Holy Spirit to produce patience in me. I feel as if I'm losing my cool over everything. I want to be patient right away—but how can I without the opportunity to practice patience? Your Word tells me that I need patient endurance to do your will. By enduring life's difficulties without becoming anxious or annoyed, I can become more patient. And as I grow in patience, my trust in you will also grow. Lord Jesus, you have answered my prayer for patience by bringing opportunities for your Holy Spirit to perfect this area in my heart. When frustrating circumstances come my way, help me to react with calm dignity and quiet strength.

Patient endurance is what you need now, so that you will continue to do God's will. Then you will receive all that he has promised. HEBREWS 10:36

☼ A prayer for RECONCILIATION
Why is reconciliation so important to God?

DEAR JESUS,

Reconciliation is the heart of what it means to follow you. You suffered the agony of the cross to redeem sinful human beings and reconcile us to God. My reconciliation with you is a picture of how I am to be reconciled with others. Your Word tells me that harmony in human relationships is important to you—so important that you command me to first come clean with the people in my life with whom I have conflict, and then to worship. In other words, to live with an unresolved conflict actually hinders my relationship with you. Jesus, is there anyone in my life with whom you want me to pursue reconciliation? I pray that you would show me how to restore that relationship so I can be at peace with you.

If you are presenting a sacrifice at the altar in the Temple and you suddenly remember that someone has something against you, leave your sacrifice there at the altar. Go and be reconciled to that person. Then come and offer your sacrifice to God. MATTHEW 5:23-24

☼ **A prayer for DISCIPLINE**
When I need to develop the discipline of obeying God

DEAR LORD,

I want to cultivate the discipline of obedience; no, I want to begin to love obeying you with all my heart. It is so difficult to make obedience to you and your Word a regular habit. I am frustrated by my constant drift toward the temptations that cause me to sin. Lord, please show me how to be inclined toward obedience, not sin. Motivate me to focus on your Scripture—to love to open its pages and meditate on its life-giving truths. Give me the desire to teach its truths to others so that I might apply them more thoroughly. Show me opportunities to talk about what you are doing in my life so that I can be a living testimony. May obedience become a path I have traveled so far that I could never go back another way.

Commit yourselves wholeheartedly to these words of mine. Tie them to your hands and wear them on your forehead as reminders. Teach them to your children. Talk about them when you are at home and when you are on the road, when you are going to bed and when you are getting up. Write them on the doorposts of your house.

DEUTERONOMY 11:18-20

☼ **A prayer for the POWER OF GOD**
When I long to experience God's power working through me

ALMIGHTY GOD,

I am trying to imagine being in the midst of the earth's strongest earthquake, tallest tsunami, wildest volcano, and most devastating hurricane—all at the same time. I'm certain this cannot even begin to compare to your power! You are the creator of all these phenomena, and what is created is never more powerful than the Creator. But you are also the same God who has the power to calm the storms in my heart, to dry up a flood of fear, to quench the lust for sin, and to control the whirlwinds in my life. Grant me the humility to put more trust in your power than my own. Don't let my resources get in the way so that I fail to rely on you. May your power flow through me like an electric current flows through a wire. The wire is simply a conductor; it has no power in itself. But without the wire, the current doesn't go anywhere. Let me be a person who is willing to be wired for your service so that I can be a conduit of your love, help, and grace to those around me.

We now have this light shining in our hearts, but we ourselves are like fragile clay jars containing this great treasure. This makes it clear that our great power is from God, not from ourselves. 2 CORINTHIANS 4:7

DAY 215

☀ **A prayer about the HOLY SPIRIT**
*When I wonder how the Holy Spirit makes
a difference in my life*

DEAR GOD,

Thank you for your Holy Spirit, who is your presence living within me, helping me discover the wonders of your character and teaching me deep truths about who you are. It is your Spirit in me that helps me know the truth about sin and convicts me when I do sin. You help me distinguish between right and wrong, good and bad, your way and the way of the world. Thank you, God, that you care enough about me to give me one-on-one instructions for how to live a life that pleases you.

I will ask the Father, and he will give you another Advocate, who will never leave you. He is the Holy Spirit, who leads into all truth. The world cannot receive him, because it isn't looking for him and doesn't recognize him. But you know him, because he lives with you now and later will be in you.
JOHN 14:16-17

☼ A prayer for FORGIVENESS
   When I need forgiveness

DEAR GOD,

I've messed up, and I expect to face the consequences.
I'm asking you to help me start over. When my heart is
sincere and I truly want forgiveness, you give me another
chance—again and again. Sometimes I wonder why. How
can you continue to forgive me? Your patient and repeated
forgiveness is proof that you desire a personal relationship
with me. Thank you that your mercy never ends.

*I—yes, I alone—will blot out your sins for my own sake and
will never think of them again.* ISAIAH 43:25

☼ A prayer in times of DEPRESSION
   *When I need to reverse the downward spiral of
   feelings that can lead to depression*

O LORD,

I feel like I am sinking lower and lower. All I can see is my
own problems, pain, and despair. The more I withdraw
into myself, the more difficult it becomes to see things
clearly. In fact, I can only look inward, at my pain. God,
I need your help to stop this negative cycle. Help me to
praise you so that I can once again see how much you care
for me. I praise you, God!

*Great is the LORD! He is most worthy of praise! He is to be
feared above all gods.* 1 CHRONICLES 16:25

☼ **A prayer about BACKSLIDING**
What do I do when I've fallen away from God?

DEAR LOVING GOD,

When it comes to my relationship with you, every day I have a choice: I can step toward you or step away from you. It takes conscious effort to step toward you; it takes no effort to step away, for my sinful nature is always pulling me in the wrong direction. Lord, suddenly I am realizing that I am farther from you than I want to be. I sense this is a critical moment: I can either deny the problem and keep going the wrong way, or I can recognize my sin and turn toward you. Please don't let me slip away any more than I have, O God. I confess all I am doing that is causing me to move away. Now may your loving forgiveness pull me back toward you so that I can walk with you now and forever.

This is what the LORD says to the family of Israel: "Come back to me and live!" AMOS 5:4

☼ **A prayer for ENDURANCE**

When I want to be effective in serving Jesus my whole life long

DEAR JESUS,

Why is it so difficult to do good over a long period of time? It is especially hard when life brings me a string of temptations. How can I be faithful even in the midst of such trials? Just when I think my faith is strong enough to endure, I give in to something I shouldn't or I'm overwhelmed by doubt. Perhaps my desires are not yet aligned with yours. Maybe I'm still hoping for things that don't produce long-term discipleship—things like status, control, or acceptance. These things won't last, so when I hope in them, I will be disappointed. Jesus, you promise me none of these things. You taught that to be the greatest, I must be willing to be the least. So instead of expecting my faith to make me great, let my faith demonstrate your greatness. When I stumble and fall, make me humble and teachable, and redeem my mistakes. Help me to persevere and refocus my hope on you.

In his kindness God called you to share in his eternal glory by means of Christ Jesus. So after you have suffered a little while, he will restore, support, and strengthen you, and he will place you on a firm foundation. 1 PETER 5:10

⚙ **A prayer about GUILT**
When I need to be free from guilt

DEAR GOD,

I have confessed my sin to you, but I still feel guilty. I know the problem is with me. But I cannot atone for my sin by feeling guilty and miserable. Part of receiving your forgiveness is trusting that I really am cleansed of my sins. Let me not only believe this but act on it, responding to your grace in every aspect of my life. Your love breaks the power of sin so that I am free to worship you gratefully, make costly sacrifices willingly, serve humbly, and express my faith boldly. Even though my feelings condemn me, I know I am forgiven. Lord, please let my faith in you overcome my feelings of guilt so I can walk in the freedom of being cleansed from every wrong.

Even if we feel guilty, God is greater than our feelings, and he knows everything. 1 JOHN 3:20

☼ **A prayer about WORRY**
*Where can I find peace when I'm overwhelmed
with worry?*

LORD GOD,

You are well aware of my anxious heart. I admit that I
worry about almost everything, and I know that's a mis-
use of the imagination you gave me. Most of the things
I worry about never even happen, so when I worry, I am
wasting my time and emotional energy for nothing. Lord,
I want to trust in you. Please change my anxious heart
into a heart at peace. When I feel consumed with worry,
remind me to turn those anxious thoughts into prayers
that lift my concerns to you. Then help me to let go of
them, realizing that there is no problem you cannot overcome. Help me to find peace knowing that you are taking
care of me. When I trust in you, I have no need to worry.
Thank you for that, Lord.

*The LORD keeps watch over you as you come and go, both
now and forever.* PSALM 121:8

☼ A prayer about ACCOMPLISHMENTS
When I want to know my accomplishments are pleasing to God

HEAVENLY FATHER,

Sometimes I assume that accomplishing great things is the way to become spiritually great. If I am honest, I am often driven to impress others or to gain their respect, applause, or approval. Striving for these things can easily transfer to my relationship with you, God, leaving me thinking that I have to earn your love and forgiveness too. But your Word tells me that I am accepted because of your grace, not because of what I do. God, you accepted me from the start, before I had accomplished anything. It's true that I have been created, called, and equipped to accomplish certain things for you. But my achievements are always to be understood as the result of your grace in me, not of my own efforts. The greatest success is allowing you to carry out your plans through me. Help me to let go of my need to be accepted because of my performance. Instead, may I accomplish those things that will highlight your power at work in me.

We are God's masterpiece. He has created us anew in Christ Jesus, so we can do the good things he planned for us long ago.
EPHESIANS 2:10

☀ **A prayer about STRENGTH**
   What is true strength in God's eyes?

DEAR GOD,

So many people think that following you means being weak. I know that's not true! It takes strength to humbly obey you when I am tempted to sin. It takes great courage to serve others through acts of kindness when I don't feel like it. But please never let me mistake raw power for true strength. Let me live by the biblical concept of strength: power under the control of love.

I take pleasure in my weaknesses, and in the insults, hardships, persecutions, and troubles that I suffer for Christ. For when I am weak, then I am strong.
2 CORINTHIANS 12:10

DAY 224 *Prayerful Moment*

☀ **A prayer about DESIRES**
   When my desires overwhelm me and I need help

DEAR GOD,

Sometimes my desires are so strong that they keep me from thinking straight. Like Samson in the Bible, I can become so obsessed with what I want that I forget to ask for your guidance and wisdom. Help me to know whether the objects of my desire are consistent with your will.

Fix your thoughts on what is true, and honorable, and right, and pure, and lovely, and admirable. Think about things that are excellent and worthy of praise. PHILIPPIANS 4:8

⚙ **A prayer about TESTING**
   Does God test the quality of my faith?

HEAVENLY FATHER,

I wish it weren't so, but I know that my character and spiritual commitment are tested by the fires of hardship and suffering. Please give me the wisdom to clearly distinguish between temptation, which Satan uses to lead me into sin, and testing, which you use to purify me and move me toward spiritual maturity. Out of testing comes a more committed faith. Just as many products are tested so that their performance can be strengthened, so also you test my faith to strengthen me and make me more like you. When my faith is being tested, may I realize you are working out something important in me so that my relationship with you, and service to you, might be more significant.

Dear brothers and sisters, when troubles come your way, consider it an opportunity for great joy. For you know that when your faith is tested, your endurance has a chance to grow. So let it grow, for when your endurance is fully developed, you will be perfect and complete, needing nothing.
JAMES 1:2-4

☼ A prayer about THOUGHTS
When I keep thinking wrong things

DEAR LORD,

Right now I am having a hard time thinking about you because so many other things crowd my thoughts. And many of those thoughts, I am embarrassed to admit, aren't pure. I know you take my thought life seriously because my thoughts reveal who I really am. And I am not the person I want to be. Lord, please help me work on changing my heart. I know my thought life will follow. May I desire the character that comes from your heart. I can begin right now by reading Scripture, meditating on it, and memorizing passages that focus on the essence of a heart committed to you. Please do your merciful work within me, helping me to desire a heart that longs for you. When I am willing, I know you can transform my thoughts.

It is what comes from inside that defiles you. . . . All these vile things come from within; they are what defile you.
MARK 7:20, 23

☼ A prayer about ENCOURAGEMENT
When I want to thank God for encouraging me

DEAR GOD,

What an encouragement it is to know that your power—
the power of the Lord of Heaven's Armies—is on my side.
The number of enemies against me doesn't matter to you.
After all, you used the young boy David to overcome the
giant Goliath. You used Gideon's three hundred soldiers to
defeat the vast armies of Midian. And you used the twelve
disciples to establish the whole church. I don't have to be
above average for you to do great things through me; in
fact, you seem to take joy in doing great works through
ordinary people. Knowing that you work through me
despite my limitations inspires me to desire to worship
and honor you.

*We also pray that you will be strengthened with all his glori-
ous power so you will have all the endurance and patience
you need. May you be filled with joy, always thanking the
Father. He has enabled you to share in the inheritance that
belongs to his people, who live in the light. For he has rescued us from the kingdom of darkness and transferred us
into the Kingdom of his dear Son, who purchased our freedom and forgave our sins.* COLOSSIANS 1:11-14

⚙ **A prayer about ETERNAL LIFE**
When I need the hope of eternal life to affect my life right now

DEAR GOD,

Your Word says that you have planted eternity in the human heart. I believe that every person, deep down, knows there is more beyond this life. Something we were made for is still missing. Because I am created in your image, I know I have eternal value. Help me to focus on things that will last forever—my relationships with you and others, my acts of service, and my words of encouragement and counsel. You have created me with a restless yearning for the kind of perfect world that can only be found in heaven. But today I can do my part to try to model the kind of life you have promised I will enjoy forever. Thank you for the glimpses of heaven you allow me to see each day through nature, art, a smile, or an act of love. Someday you will restore earth, and eternity will be a never-ending exploration of its beauty in a perfect relationship with you. But now, through my obedience to you and love for you, I can put myself in a position to enjoy life the way it is meant to be enjoyed. My relationships can be more faithful, my life can model integrity, and my conscience can be clear. May the people I come into contact with today notice the eternity you have planted in me and desire it.

No eye has seen, no ear has heard, and no mind has imagined what God has prepared for those who love him.
1 CORINTHIANS 2:9

✦ A prayer when in CRISIS
If I'm obeying God, why am I going through such difficult times?

DEAR JESUS,

The disciples were your devoted followers, yet they seemed so surprised when a dangerous storm on the Sea of Galilee threatened their lives. Perhaps they thought that being your followers excluded them from facing life's trials. I sometimes have this same expectation. Yet in the midst of a crisis, the disciples still knew where to turn for help. Their story is proof that even the most spiritually hardy still face crises that shake them to the core. Just as the disciples called out to you for rescue, I know I can call out to you when I face my own life storms. Although the raging storm didn't awaken you, the disciples' cries of need roused you immediately. Like a mother who can hear her child's cry over the din of a crowd, your ear is attuned to me, Jesus. You are tireless as you care for me. When I call out to you, your presence breaks through my fears and calms my heart, even as the storms of life continue to rage around me.

Call on me when you are in trouble, and I will rescue you, and you will give me glory. PSALM 50:15

☼ A prayer when in difficult CIRCUMSTANCES
When I start to panic, I can turn to God in prayer

DEAR JESUS,

When I'm tempted to panic, instead I run to you in prayer, because I refuse to worry. When bad circumstances come my way, one of the hardest lessons for me is to turn my worries into confident prayers. But you know my needs, and you have never failed to meet them. I know you can be trusted to bring good fruit out of these hard times.

Don't worry about anything; instead, pray about everything. Tell God what you need, and thank him for all he has done.
PHILIPPIANS 4:6

DAY 231 *Prayerful Moment*

☼ A prayer for SPIRITUAL GROWTH
When I want to mature in my faith

LORD,

Few things are more glorious than a beautiful sunrise. As that yellow ball rises above the horizon, it promises a new day with new beginnings and new opportunities. Likewise, my relationship with you is the source of my daily strength in every situation. Your love and care for me warms my soul and gives me hope. As I commit my life to you, please shine your glory through me more and more.

The way of the righteous is like the first gleam of dawn, which shines ever brighter until the full light of day.
PROVERBS 4:18

✸ **A prayer when in CONFLICT**
When I face a difficult conflict

O LORD,

I need help resolving a conflict. Neither side wants to budge, but I know that someone must make the first move. Let it be me. Teach me humility, that I might prefer peace over personal victory. Give me the discernment to know where to compromise, to locate common ground that is greater than our differences, and to give up ground for no reason other than love. If neither I nor my friend is willing to take the initiative to accomplish a resolution, I'm afraid this conflict will result in a broken relationship. And what are we really fighting over? Mostly our pride. Lord, you are the great peacemaker. Please lead us to peace. And like you, may I be willing to give up my rights to gain the right to be called a peacemaker.

You have heard the law that says, "Love your neighbor" and hate your enemy. But I say, love your enemies! Pray for those who persecute you! In that way, you will be acting as true children of your Father in heaven. MATTHEW 5:43-45

☼ A prayer about NEGLECT
When I've been avoiding God

LORD,

I have been neglectful of you and many of the things you have asked me to do. I often use the same excuse, claiming that it doesn't feel like the right time to start the practice of daily Bible study, to begin tithing, to share the gospel with a non-Christian friend, or to stop a sinful habit. If I'm honest with myself, my issue isn't timing—it's priority. Lord, I see now that any excuse for neglecting my relationship with you is merely a cloak for a fearful spirit or a stubborn heart. Forgive me for abandoning you and the responsibilities and privileges that come from being a part of your family. Where my spirit is fearful, restore my trust in you. Where my heart is stubborn, soften it for you. Instead of making excuses, I want to be devoted to serving you. Help me understand what things compete for priority in my life. May we together root them out so that you will regain your rightful place in my heart—as my number one priority.

Seek the Kingdom of God above all else, and live righteously, and he will give you everything you need.
MATTHEW 6:33

☼ A prayer about DOUBT
Can God use me, even when I doubt myself?

DEAR GOD,

I can relate to Moses when you called him to deliver the Israelites from Egypt. He was certain he could not do what you were asking. The task was too big, and he was scared, unprepared, and full of doubt. This is how I feel right now—frightened to death, totally unprepared, and doubtful that you've called the right person. But the story of Moses gives me hope because it shows that you work through humble hearts that depend on you. Like Moses, I have a realistic picture of my limitations and abilities. I know I can't do this job by my own skill. I have two choices: walk away, or let you work through me. I want to follow in Moses' footsteps. May I have courage when the task ahead of me seems too big. When I doubt my ability to see it through, may I persevere in the knowledge that where you call, you provide. Lord, I'm totally depending on you. I'm frightened, unequipped, and doubtful . . . but I'm willing. I trust you to work through me.

He gives power to the weak and strength to the powerless.
ISAIAH 40:29

⚙ **A prayer about CREATIVITY**
*How can the workmanship of God spark my
own creativity?*

HEAVENLY FATHER, MAKER OF HEAVEN AND
EARTH,

Nature displays beauty that surpasses the finest music,
poetry, or creative genius of all human artists put together.
You are the Creator. You are a God of design, color, plan,
organization, beauty, magnificence, and order. The great
art of the world only copies your splendid creation. The
finest model of craftsmanship and artistic skill is found in
the creation of the universe. Any creativity I posses is the
overflow of a mind filled with the good things you have
made, O God. When I'm looking for inspiration, I will
fill my heart with your creative wonders. Let my creative
expression be glorifying to you, my God and my Maker.

*The heavens proclaim the glory of God. The skies display his
craftsmanship. Day after day they continue to speak; night
after night they make him known. They speak without a
sound or word; their voice is never heard. Yet their message
has gone throughout the earth, and their words to all
the world.* PSALM 19:1-4

☀ A prayer for CONVERSATION
Can I live my life in conversation with God?

DEAR GOD,

I would love to be like your servant Nehemiah, who lived with a constant sense of your presence. Your Word shows that his life was a moment-by-moment conversation with you, even as he pursued his ambitious agenda to rebuild the protective walls of Jerusalem. How can I grow more aware of you speaking in my life? Perhaps I could put a Post-it note on my computer to remind me to breathe a quick prayer whenever I sit down to work. Or I could set my cell-phone alarm to sound every sixty minutes, and then take thirty seconds to review how you have been with me the last hour and ask you to help me in the hour ahead. The point is, I need to take time to listen to you so our relationship can grow. Or really, so that I will grow closer to you as I settle myself and listen for your voice. My spiritual maturity is often hindered by inattention. I show up, but I come with an agenda and a list of demands. I'm sorry, God. I'm tired of my own voice, and I want to hear yours. Please talk to me. I'm ready to listen. Show me how my life can become a moment-by-moment conversation with you.

Come and listen to my counsel. I'll share my heart with you and make you wise. PROVERBS 1:23

☼ A prayer about LISTENING
What are the blessings of being a good listener?

DEAR JESUS,

Teach me to be a better listener. Soften my heart so that I may receive counsel willingly and with gratitude. When I stumble or make mistakes, give me the humility to accept godly correction so that I may grow in understanding. As I learn to be a good listener, I pray that you would bring me the blessings of spiritual maturity.

If you listen to correction, you grow in understanding.
PROVERBS 15:32

DAY 238 *Prayerful Moment*

☼ A prayer for INTEGRITY
When I want to live with great integrity

DEAR LORD,

I want to live a life of integrity! I want consistency between what I believe and how I live. I want to apply the truth of your Word to every aspect of my life. I want to model your character in every word and action. May your priorities become mine. As I set these high standards, help me remember that I don't have to be perfect. Instead, teach me to trust you so that the integrity of your character will be seen in my life every day.

The LORD rewarded me for doing right. He has seen my innocence. To the faithful you show yourself faithful; to those with integrity you show integrity. PSALM 18:24-25

⚙ **A prayer about CRITICISM**
When I need a more teachable heart

O GOD,

I confess I do not take criticism well. I'm so quick to defend myself or prove myself right. But your Word says that rejecting correction is the hallmark of a fool, and a core attribute of wisdom is a teachable heart. That's what I need—a teachable heart. Why am I always convinced that my way is best or my opinion is right? How often have I dismissed helpful criticism because I didn't want to admit I could be wrong? I know that comes from my stubborn human nature. But what if I looked at advice as a guidepost to keep me from pursuing the wrong path? O God, humble me so I can hear your voice—whether through the gentle rebuke of a trusted friend or in the advice of godly people. I'm listening, God, and I trust that you will help me discern wise correction. Please don't allow my wounded pride to reject constructive criticism that will help me grow.

Fools think their own way is right, but the wise listen to others. A fool is quick-tempered, but a wise person stays calm when insulted. An honest witness tells the truth; a false witness tells lies. Some people make cutting remarks, but the words of the wise bring healing. PROVERBS 12:15-18

A prayer about ADVERSITY
When God feels far away

DEAR GOD,

Sometimes when I am faced with great adversity I feel like asking, "Where are you when I need you most?" But I know the answer is always the same—you are right beside me. You are here, providing the power to help me cope. Isaiah 43:2 says, "*When* you go through deep waters, I will be with you," so I understand that you don't promise to remove all my troubles. Adversity is a natural consequence of living in a fallen world. Lord, I understand that if you always kept me from struggle or granted my every wish, I would follow you for the wrong reasons. But I thank you that my struggles are not wasted. You use them to sharpen my character and strengthen my faith in you. I take comfort in your promises to be with me *in* my troubles and to give me wisdom to cope, strength to conquer my problems, and understanding to see how I might become stronger as I learn to trust you.

The LORD is good, a strong refuge when trouble comes. He is close to those who trust in him. NAHUM 1:7

☼ **A prayer about DECISIONS**
When I need affirmation that my little decisions really matter

FATHER IN HEAVEN,

Thank you that object lessons from everyday life can teach me about following you, the holy God. Today as I walked, it occurred to me that making right decisions is like hiking; each step puts me a little further down the path. It struck me that making the right decision simply means being faithful in little things—one small step at a time. Your will for me is first and foremost to read the Bible, obey you, serve others, and do what is right. If I decide simply to do that today and each day, I can be sure that I will be doing your will tomorrow and twenty years from now. Then when I approach the end of my life on earth, I will leave behind a legacy of faithfulness. Father, please help me with the first small step.

My steps have stayed on your path; I have not wavered from following you. PSALM 17:5

✦ A prayer when in DANGER
When temptation becomes increasingly threatening

DEAR GOD,

Please protect me from the temptation to do wrong. That is one danger I face constantly. How grateful I am when I see a guardrail along a dangerous curve in the road. I know it's there not to inhibit my freedom to drive but to save my life if I lose control. Please give me the wisdom to recognize the guardrails you have set up to protect me as I travel through life. May I feel security and relief when I see them, rather than frustration that my freedom might be inhibited. And may I remember to thank you when one of those guardrails saves me from disaster. As I travel this life journey, may I rely on your Word to guard my heart so that I can stay focused on the road you have mapped out for me. Perhaps more than anything else this will prevent me from having a terrible accident when temptation tries to distract me.

Stay alert! Watch out for your great enemy, the devil. He prowls around like a roaring lion, looking for someone to devour. 1 PETER 5:8

DAY 243

☀ A prayer about ABILITIES
When I doubt I am up to the task

LORD,

Deep within the human spirit lies a longing and a capacity to do significant things. Because I am made in your image, God, I have inherited from you the desire to create, to accomplish, to make things happen. You wouldn't have given me these desires without the abilities to carry them out. My abilities are gifts from you to help me accomplish great things in your name. How I use my abilities ultimately determines my quality of life—not defined by comfort or the accumulation of wealth, but by strong character, joy, and lasting satisfaction. Lord, you desire that I focus on discovering my abilities, developing them, and channeling them toward what will achieve the greatest good for those around me. Thank you, Lord, that when you ask me to accomplish something, you give me the resources to get the job done.

God has given us different gifts for doing certain things well.
ROMANS 12:6

☀ A prayer about COMPLIMENTS
How can my compliments help others experience divine encouragement?

DEAR GOD,

Why am I so stingy with my compliments? Even worse, why do I sometimes only compliment someone to receive a compliment in return? I know that genuine praise, from a pure and tender heart, can provide great encouragement to others. How often have I been affirmed by something that someone said? May I be such an encouragement in the lives of my family and friends!

The words of the godly are a life-giving fountain; the words of the wicked conceal violent intentions. PROVERBS 10:11

DAY 245 *Prayerful Moment*

☀ A prayer for IMPACT
When I want to have an impact on those around me

DEAR LORD,

The more I am able to reflect your character, the more people will be drawn to what is different about me and the more opportunity I will have to tell them how you have changed my life. Though I will always make plenty of mistakes, my goal is to live in such a way that people will clearly see your life in me. O Lord, may it be so.

Let your good deeds shine out for all to see, so that everyone will praise your heavenly Father. MATTHEW 5:16

⚙ A prayer about INVOLVEMENT
When getting involved feels too complicated

GOD,

These days I seem to find it increasingly easy to say, "I don't want to get involved." Maybe my excuse is that the situation looks too messy or complicated. Often, when I see someone in need or notice something I could do to help, I am tempted to turn a blind eye. I sometimes hope someone else will do something about it. But God, you remind me that I am to be compassionate and active, ready and willing to go the extra mile. Your command to love my neighbor is a command to take action. You don't tell me to love my neighbor when it's convenient; you tell me to make the most of every opportunity. Opportunities to get involved are also your way of getting my attention. It is amazing how one of the best ways to experience your presence, God, is by getting involved in the lives of others! Show me where I need to be involved today.

Now I am giving you a new commandment: Love each other. Just as I have loved you, you should love each other. Your love for one another will prove to the world that you are my disciples. JOHN 13:34-35

☀ **A prayer for PURPOSE**
When I need a dream to follow

O GOD,

I'm amazed to know that you created me for a purpose.
It only makes sense that you, my Creator, know exactly
what will satisfy the longings of my heart. But I have a
choice: either I follow you and do what you already know
will fulfill me and make a difference in this world, or I
choose to go my own way. O Lord, I choose to pursue
your plan for me because that is the only way I can be sure
that my life will have meaning. I choose you and want to
accomplish what you created me to do. Could life be more
meaningful? I understand that it may take years to fulfill
your plans, God. But I will never stop searching because
the searching keeps me close to you.

*You made all the delicate, inner parts of my body and knit
me together in my mother's womb. . . . You saw me before I
was born. Every day of my life was recorded in your book.
Every moment was laid out before a single day had passed.
How precious are your thoughts about me, O God. They
cannot be numbered!* PSALM 139:13, 16-17

☀ A prayer for ACCOUNTABILITY
When I don't want accountability, but I need it

DEAR GOD,

You know my secret habits and private thoughts that I wouldn't dare share with anyone else. But that's the problem, isn't it? To break free from what I keep in the hidden places of my heart, I need to expose the darkness in me to the spotlight of your truth. When things are out in the open, I will have to deal with them. Please give me the courage to be accountable, not only for what I do, but for my thoughts and attitudes. I know this will be painful, but if I have no accountability, I will continue to sink into more destructive thoughts and habits. My secret sins will eat away at my character and integrity until my reputation crashes down around me. Without accountability, I wouldn't even see it coming. And so, Lord, please send me a wise friend or mentor to keep me accountable. Don't let the darkness take over my heart. I want to live in your light.

If another believer is overcome by some sin, you who are godly should gently and humbly help that person back onto the right path. And be careful not to fall into the same temptation yourself. Share each other's burdens.

GALATIANS 6:1-2

☀ A prayer of SELF-DENIAL
Am I willing to make sacrifices to follow Jesus?

DEAR JESUS,

You call me to take up my cross and follow you. Oh, how I want to follow you. But I need your help to break the self-centered desires that tie me to this world. Motivate me to exercise self-discipline in the way I live. Give me the willingness to deny self-centered attitudes for the sake of obeying you. Provide me with the courage to give up some things that are getting in the way of my obedience. Jesus, if you asked me, would I be willing to give up everything for you? Oh, I hope my answer would be yes. Though you may never ask that, please produce in me the willing attitude that you love so much in those who follow you.

Jesus said to his disciples, "If any of you wants to be my follower, you must turn from your selfish ways, take up your cross, and follow me. If you try to hang on to your life, you will lose it. But if you give up your life for my sake, you will save it." MATTHEW 16:24-25

⚙ **A prayer about the PROMISES OF GOD**
When I need to cling to the promises of God

LORD OF HEAVEN AND EARTH,

How could I have any hope without your promises? I cling to so many. You promise salvation to all who accept the gift. You promise to be with me in the form of the Holy Spirit. You promise to forgive me whenever I do wrong, if I just ask you. And you promise that nothing I do is beyond your forgiveness. You promise peace of heart and mind when I entrust my life to you. You promise to use even the bad things that happen to me for good purposes. And best of all, you promise that Jesus is coming back to judge the world and to bring your followers into your presence forever. I praise you for your wonderful promises, Lord! May I now promise to follow and worship you, the one who always keeps his promises.

Deep in your hearts you know that every promise of the LORD your God has come true. Not a single one has failed! JOSHUA 23:14

⚙ **A prayer about CHANGE**
When life takes a turn for the worse

DEAR GOD,

Sometimes the changes in my life seem to be for the worse, and I get discouraged. When that happens, it helps to remember Joseph, who was sold by his own brothers into slavery, but who later became governor of all of Egypt and saved many people from starvation. The next time change makes me feel like I'm going to fall apart, remind me that even traumatic, unpredictable, and unfair changes will never trump your will. Help me to trust that you will take the bad situations in my life and turn them into something good.

I am the LORD, and I do not change. MALACHI 3:6

DAY 252 *Prayerful Moment*

⚙ **A prayer about IRRITATION**
When I'm ready to explode in anger

LORD,

I'm irritated. But before I take out my irritation on others, help me to pause and respond in love instead. When I want to lash out, overwhelm me with the power of your love. Keep me from saying something I will later regret. Teach me to treat others with love so that I can continue to be a credible witness for you.

Sensible people control their temper; they earn respect by overlooking wrongs. PROVERBS 19:11

☼ **A prayer about RELATIONSHIP**
When guilt causes me to hide to from God

DEAR GOD,

Like Adam and Eve, my first response after disobeying you is to try to hide. And yet, after they sinned, the first thing you did was to pursue them. Even though their actions had severe consequences and forever changed the way they related to you, the Bible makes clear that you had no intention of completely severing your relationship with them over sin. Could you feel the same for me? Even though I try to conceal myself, do you come to search me out? It is hard to understand that kind of unconditional love, but I'm so thankful that you never give up on me after I've disobeyed you. I often try to hide because I feel guilt over what I've done, but now I understand that you allow me to experience those emotions so I will realize my sin and ask for your forgiveness. Guilt is not meant to drive me away from you but to bring me back into relationship with you. Your faithful pursuit of me is a beautiful call to friendship with you. Next time I feel guilt over my disobedience, please remind me to run . . . straight back to you!

The kind of sorrow God wants us to experience leads us away from sin and results in salvation. There's no regret for that kind of sorrow. But worldly sorrow, which lacks repentance, results in spiritual death. 2 CORINTHIANS 7:10

DAY 254

☀ **A prayer in CRISIS**
Where is God in times of crisis?

LORD GOD,

I don't need to pray that you will be with me in this time of crisis, because you are already here. Instead I ask, Lord, that I will recognize your presence and have the humility to accept your help. You do not promise to prevent times of crisis in my life; this is a fallen world where terrible things happen. But you do promise to be here with me and for me—always—helping me through any crisis I face. You promise to guide me toward peace and hope in the midst of my crisis. You also promise to bring me to heaven, where all trouble will end forever. Help me to cling to your promises as I trust in your presence to carry me through each crisis I face.

Can anything ever separate us from Christ's love? Does it mean he no longer loves us if we have trouble or calamity, or are persecuted, or hungry, or destitute, or in danger, or threatened with death? . . . No, despite all these things, overwhelming victory is ours through Christ, who loved us.
ROMANS 8:35, 37

⚙ **A prayer about CHOICES**
   When I need guidance to make the right choices

DEAR JESUS,

Each day presents me with many choices. The best choices I can make are to honor you and obey your Word, because doing that will always put me squarely in the center of your will. I pray that you will direct me in my decision making. Teach me as I read your Word, guide me as I communicate with you in prayer, and speak to me through the advice of godly friends and mentors. Keep me from choices that benefit me at the expense of others. It's such a simple guideline to put others before myself and put you before everything else, but implementing it can be challenging. Each day offers me the choice to serve you, Lord. Please help me to maintain a "God first" attitude so I can know with certainty that I am choosing your ways.

He guides me along right paths, bringing honor to his name.
PSALM 23:3

☼ A prayer about DESIRES
When I wonder if it is okay to want something

DEAR LORD,

Is it okay to really want something? Did you create my desires as a way for me to express myself, or are they wrong and selfish? Lord, may my desires be fueled by right motives and directed toward things that are good, right, and God honoring. Then I will know they must be okay. For example, I can see that the desire to love is healthy and right when it is directed toward my spouse. But that same desire for sexual intimacy directed toward anyone else would be adultery. The desire to lead an organization is healthy if my motive is to serve others, but wrong if my motive is to gain control over others. May my greatest desire be for a close relationship with you, O God, for I know this will influence all my other desires.

I desire you more than anything on earth. PSALM 73:25

⚙ **A prayer about CRISIS**
When I want my response to a crisis to reveal my faith

LORD,

Too often a crisis exposes my unbelief and fear rather than my confidence in you. In spite of everything you have done for me in the past, I still have trouble trusting you to deliver me this time. The crisis I now see looks more powerful than the God I cannot see. Please allow your faithfulness in the past to bolster my faith that you will deliver me now. In this time of crisis, O God, motivate me to turn toward you. For when I look at you, I will learn from you and cling to you. How else can I make it through this difficult time with wisdom, grace, and peace? May this crisis convince me of your presence and empower me with your salvation so that my faith may be an encouragement to others.

God is our refuge and strength, always ready to help in times of trouble. So we will not fear when earthquakes come and the mountains crumble into the sea. Let the oceans roar and foam. Let the mountains tremble as the waters surge!
PSALM 46:1-3

❄ **A prayer of HOPE**
When I place my hope in God

DEAR GOD,

When it feels as if everything is falling apart, I will cling to the fact that you keep your word. One thing you have promised is that, in heaven, all suffering will cease. Never again will we grieve or be discouraged. I praise you for that! Help me to trust that you will either deliver me from these tough times or see me through for your own glory.

Let us hold tightly without wavering to the hope we affirm, for God can be trusted to keep his promise.
HEBREWS 10:23

DAY 259 *Prayerful Moment*

❄ **A prayer about LISTENING**
When I wish God would speak to me

DEAR GOD,

You speak to me in many ways, but to hear you, I must pay attention. When I come before you daily, help me to use this special time to be still and to wait expectantly for you to speak. Teach me to pay attention, and help me to carve out times when I can listen to you. Don't let me miss an opportunity for a lesson from you, the master teacher. Teach me to hear you more and more as I take time to pause and listen for your voice.

Be still, and know that I am God! PSALM 46:10

⚙ **A prayer about DEATH**
When I'm afraid of dying

GOD IN HEAVEN,

I am so afraid of dying. While this life is often scary and hard, it is all I know. The uncertainty of death is what terrifies me most. God, I believe in your Son, Jesus, and I know I will be in heaven when this life is over. So why am I afraid? If I could see from your perspective, would I live in constant fear of death? I trust your assurances that I will have an eternal future, but maybe I don't know enough about it. As I read your Word, teach me about my eternal home in heaven and what it will be like. I pray that you and all of your promises would become very real to me so that I will focus less on dying and more on my hope for life after death. O God, help me conquer this fear and live with joyful expectation even when the time of my death comes.

Since you have been raised to new life with Christ, set your sights on the realities of heaven. . . . Think about the things of heaven, not the things of earth. COLOSSIANS 3:1-2

☀ **A prayer about INSECURITY**
When my insecurities keep me from serving God

DEAR GOD,

How amazing that you made me in your own image. You must value me highly! You didn't make a mistake with me; you created me with unique gifts so I can do the specific tasks you have for me. You do not expect more than you know I can give, but you do insist that I use what you have given me. Help me to discover my own special gifts and then find the right area of service to use them. Just knowing your purpose for me melts away my insecurities and gives me the courage to be bold in serving you. Don't let me hesitate because of self-doubt, but help me to serve you with passion and great joy!

You have not received a spirit that makes you fearful slaves. Instead, you received God's Spirit when he adopted you as his own children. Now we call him, "Abba, Father." For his Spirit joins with our spirit to affirm that we are God's children. ROMANS 8:15-16

☀ A prayer about RELEVANCE
When others challenge the relevance of the Bible

GOD,

Many people today see the Bible as a historical work of fiction. But your Word has stood the test of time better than any other document in human history. Over several centuries, you inspired a select number of people to write down what you wanted to reveal to us about yourself and how you expect us to live. It is your love letter to us, your people. Your words have been faithfully preserved because they are your messages to people in all times and places. You will not let them disappear from the face of the earth or allow them to be altered by human hands. Because the Bible is a story of your love for all creation, it applies to all generations, cultures, and social classes. And even more astounding, it also speaks to each of us individually. Your Word offers wisdom about everything, from the practical matters of daily life to the eternal matters of the heart. It is relevant because it gives me a picture of who you are and what you have in store for me when I trust and follow you. No other book is as deeply life changing as the Bible, your inspired Word. Thank you, God, that each time I read the Bible, I learn more about how I fit into your miraculous love story.

The grass withers and the flowers fade, but the word of our God stands forever. ISAIAH 40:8

☼ **A prayer about GRIEF**
  When I am grieving

DEAR JESUS,

I am grieving a huge loss in my life. This process is not swift, nor is it a steady progression. Even after a good week, a good laugh, a theological insight, or a renewal of hope, I start to weep again. I know this is part of getting through a major life change, but I can't help but feel that there is something wrong with me. Lord Jesus, please remind me that healing is taking place and that I need to allow myself time to grieve. Some days are so difficult, and I wonder if I'll ever fully heal. When the dark days come, remind me that you are by my side and that you care about my pain. When I am full of despair, please carry me. Lord, comfort me in my grief and heal my heart. I am trusting in you to see me through this difficult time.

I will never forget this awful time, as I grieve over my loss. Yet I still dare to hope when I remember this: The faithful love of the LORD never ends! His mercies never cease. Great is his faithfulness; his mercies begin afresh each morning.
LAMENTATIONS 3:20-23

☀ **A prayer about COMPLACENCY**
How can I combat complacent inaction?

MIGHTY GOD,

In Psalm 59, David prayed that you would not destroy Israel's enemies. Why would he pray for that? Perhaps because he knew that the absence of enemies would cause the Israelites to become spiritually complacent. The threat of attack was what kept them dependent on you. I need to take this lesson to heart. I want to feel spiritually invincible, but maybe that is unhealthy for me. If I'm honest, I realize that problems keep me spiritually sharp and fully dependent on you. During good times, make me alert to the constant threat of temptation, and remind me that health, relationships, financial stability, and all other earthly blessings can vanish in an instant. The fragility of life prompts faith, and faith in you is my only true security, Lord.

In his unfailing love, my God will stand with me. He will let me look down in triumph on all my enemies. Don't kill them, for my people soon forget such lessons; stagger them with your power, and bring them to their knees, O Lord our shield. PSALM 59:10-11

☼ A prayer of DEPENDENCE
My strength comes from depending on God

ALMIGHTY GOD,

Though I've tried depending on myself and on other people and things, I now realize that nothing makes me stronger than total reliance on you. Your Spirit is always with me, helping and guiding. When I humble myself and depend on you, you strengthen my character. When I am weak, you provide the strength I need. May I always remember that you are my foundation, my rock, and the strength of my heart.

I know the LORD is always with me. I will not be shaken, for he is right beside me. PSALM 16:8

DAY 266 *Prayerful Moment*

☼ A prayer about LOSS
When I've lost someone I love

DEAR GOD,

I am still mourning my great loss. I'm grieving, and it's so difficult. Thank you, Lord, that expressing my pain is healthy and can actually bring me closer to you. Thank you that you are compassionate and patient. Please help me to feel the comfort of your presence as I move through this time of grief.

God blesses those who mourn, for they will be comforted. MATTHEW 5:4

☼ **A prayer about the FUTURE**
*When I wonder why God doesn't show me more
of the future*

O LORD,

Thank you that you reveal just enough of the future to give me hope. (You tell me that, since I'm a believer, my future in heaven will be more wonderful than I can imagine.) Thank you that you reveal just enough of the future to encourage me to obey. (To receive your rewards in the future requires my obedience in the present.) Thank you that you reveal just enough of the future to increase my dependence on you. (Since you alone know everything about the future, I must rely on you to lead me there.) Moving forward with just a glimpse of what's ahead is the essence of what it means to live by faith. Perhaps knowing more details about the future would be too much for me to take in, so I will walk with you a step at a time, staying within the light of your presence and trusting where you lead.

You guide me with your counsel, leading me to a glorious destiny. PSALM 73:24

☼ A prayer about the ARMOR OF GOD
When I need protection from spiritual attacks

ALMIGHTY GOD,

As I experience spiritual warfare, help me stand my ground against Satan through the mighty power of Jesus Christ in me. May I see beyond my human enemies to the real spiritual enemy, whom I cannot fight by myself. I must use the armor you have given me to resist his attacks. Right now I feel especially prone to spiritual attack. I need all of your armor! If Satan can conquer my heart and turn me against you, how will I be able to influence others to stay strong in the faith? Lord, I want to be a person of peace, but in this case I must fight with all my strength and use every available weapon you have given me. I cannot completely defeat Satan while I live on this earth, but I can resist him. The enemy specializes in putting obstacles in my path, but you, O God, specialize in helping me overcome them. I pray that you will equip me for battle, so that I will be victorious both in this life and in eternity.

Be strong in the Lord and in his mighty power. Put on all of God's armor so that you will be able to stand firm against all strategies of the devil. EPHESIANS 6:10-11

DAY 269

☀ A prayer about DISCOURAGEMENT
When my discouragement is overwhelming

DEAR LORD,

What is facing me seems overwhelming, if not impossible to overcome. I feel sick, embarrassed, ashamed. I have failed those I love. I am deeply discouraged and want to give up right here and right now. I simply can't see the way back to joy and happiness. Now I've got to decide: Am I going to sink yet deeper into the mire, or am I willing to begin my climb out of the pit? O God, help me! You are the balm that will heal my discouragement. You are my greatest encourager. You never abandon me, and you heal my wounds. You inspire me with your Word; you listen to my prayers and answer them in the way that is best; you revive me with hope. May your encouragement transform me again into a person of hope. May I have the strength to put my past behind me and realize that I am a forgiven person, clothed in dignity, and you count me worthy to be called your own.

From the depths of despair, O LORD, I call for your help. . . .
You encourage me by giving me strength.
PSALMS 130:1; 138:3

☼ A prayer about DIFFERENCES

How can I have harmony with people who are so different from me?

DEAR GOD,

There are so many people about whom I'd say, "We're as different as night and day." But until now, I've never thought about how that might be a good thing. In your infinite wisdom, you made light and darkness work together to form one day. Both are necessary because each facilitates life in a different way. Just as light and dark are different but united, I can be united with people who are different from me by using our differences to accomplish something whole. That can be a wonderful picture of harmony. I want to see this in action! May you provide me the opportunity to find harmony with new and different people.

There are different kinds of spiritual gifts, but the same Spirit is the source of them all. There are different kinds of service, but we serve the same Lord. God works in different ways, but it is the same God who does the work in all of us.
I CORINTHIANS 12:4-6

❋ **A prayer about PRAYER**
When I desire to have a conversation with God

DEAR GOD,

This is our time to talk together. I've come to love these times because you've taught me that there is so much more to prayer than just getting an answer to a question or a solution for a problem. My heart is often more changed through the act of praying than it is by the answer I receive. Thank you that I can be raw before you, and I often am as I honestly pour out my heart to you, confess my sins, express my pain and frustrations, make requests, and share what is happening in my life. Just telling you how I feel often makes me feel closer to you. Sometimes you lead me to praise you by showing me all you've done in my life or by teaching me about yourself. But God, you've also shown me that good conversation includes listening. When I stop and listen, you have the opportunity to share your wisdom with me, and I often gain a greater understanding of myself, my situation, my motivation, your nature, and your direction for my life. Before I end this prayer, I will take a few moments to listen respectfully for your voice. Whether or not you speak to me now, I will be thankful that you are here to share in this moment.

Don't worry about anything; instead, pray about everything. Tell God what you need, and thank him for all he has done. Then you will experience God's peace, which exceeds anything we can understand. His peace will guard your hearts and minds as you live in Christ Jesus. PHILIPPIANS 4:6-7

✳ **A prayer in BUSYNESS**
When I'm overcommitted in my activities

DEAR GOD,

I try to balance my schedule, but I fear I have overcommitted myself once again. I have fallen in the trap of busyness. Help me to overcome this tendency to be overly busy. It really is an empty way of life, and it keeps me from being fully productive for you. Give me a clear sense of your calling and the wisdom to know which things are worth doing and which things I should pass up. Empower me to make the most of the time you've given me.

Teach us to realize the brevity of life, so that we may grow in wisdom. PSALM 90:12

DAY 273 *Prayerful Moment*

✳ **A prayer about being PURSUED BY GOD**
Why does God pursue me?

HEAVENLY FATHER,

The Bible says that you desire a relationship with every person you have created. Your love relentlessly calls us to turn away from sin and toward an eternal relationship with you. Though you want us to respond positively, you graciously allow us the freedom to choose whether to return your love. Lord, I am captivated by your pursuit of me.

Long ago the LORD said to Israel: "I have loved you, my people, with an everlasting love. With unfailing love I have drawn you to myself." JEREMIAH 31:3

☼ A prayer about CONFESSION
*Why confession is essential to my relationship
with God*

O LORD,

I confess my sin to you. In humility I admit my wrong.
Against you, O God, and your standards of holiness I have
fallen short. I acknowledge the ugliness of my own sin.
Now, please help me to be humble enough to confess to
those I have hurt, even though it will be embarrassing and
painful. Confession is a necessary part of knowing you,
receiving your forgiveness, being released from guilt, and
finding a new start. It is only through the humility of
admitting my sin that I can establish honesty and trust
with you. And I know that only through confession am I
forgiven and freed from the eternal consequences of sin.
Thank you for showing me that through confession, I can
maintain an open line of communication with you.

*Finally, I confessed all my sins to you and stopped trying to
hide my guilt. I said to myself, "I will confess my rebellion
to the LORD." And you forgave me! All my guilt is gone.*
PSALM 32:5

☀ A prayer about the CALL OF GOD
How can I know what my calling is?

DEAR GOD,

What is my calling? Have you made me for a special purpose? Your Word tells me this is true. The more I get to know you through reading the Bible, the more I sense that you have something special in store for my life. As I read your Word, please bless me with the knowledge of what you want me to do and where you want me to go. Bring me insight into how you made me so I can see where I might fit in your plan. Your Word tells me that you give each person certain aptitudes. Help me to develop my abilities so that I can use them for you. Your Word also tells me that when you transform me by the power of your Holy Spirit, you will literally change the way I think. May my transformed mind recognize your leading. Please don't let me miss your calling because I wasn't ready or I didn't recognize it. Instead, when your calling comes, let it fill my thoughts and consume my energies so that I long to pursue it wholeheartedly.

Your word is a lamp to guide my feet and a light for my path.
PSALM 119:105

☼ A prayer for CONFIDENCE
When I need a healthy dose of confidence

DEAR JESUS,

I want to be confident. I don't want to be cocky, but I long to have the kind of confidence that comes from an inner assurance that I belong to you. Father, please keep me from pride and boasting. That will only make me more insecure and fearful that I will lose face in front of others. Dear Jesus, give me the inner assurance that comes from security in you—knowing that you called me for a specific purpose and have equipped me with the spiritual gifts I need to carry out that purpose. With you by my side, I can boldly set out to do your work, confident that I am within your will.

Good comes to those who lend money generously and conduct their business fairly. Such people will not be overcome by evil. Those who are righteous will be long remembered. They do not fear bad news; they confidently trust the LORD to care for them. They are confident and fearless and can face their foes triumphantly. PSALM 112:5-8

☼ A prayer about GOD'S WILL
When God's will for me seems vague

DEAR LORD,

Sometimes your will for me seems so hard to know. Perhaps the problem is that too often I'm expecting you to reveal something special to me, and I ignore the revelation you've already given in your Word. Every page of the Bible contains guidance about what you want from me: worship only you, love my neighbors and my enemies, use my spiritual gifts, tell the truth, do not covet, do not steal, be sexually pure, don't gossip, be generous, don't take your name in vain, don't let money control me, let the Holy Spirit control me instead. And there is so much more! I'm beginning to understand that doing all these things is a big part of your will for my life. I believe you also created me for a specific purpose, but until that becomes clear to me, may I follow the areas you have already laid out. As I wait for you to reveal what you want me specifically to do, strengthen me to be obedient to the things you call every person to do. Then, if I happen to miss your direction for a specific task, I won't have missed your direction for everyday life. May I never forget that obedience to your Word is your will for me.

The LORD says, "I will guide you along the best pathway for your life. I will advise you and watch over you."
PSALM 32:8

☼ A prayer about WORSHIP
When my worship feels disconnected from God

HEAVENLY FATHER,

I'm sorry that my worship over the years has not always been glorifying to you. I used to think that worship was confined to formal times and places. But now I realize that you want me to worship you according to your true person and nature, in truth and with my whole spirit. I can do that anytime and anywhere! How meaningful it is that my whole life can be an act of worship. Now, as I think about how each part of my day can glorify you, I am amazed at how often I feel connected with you. On Sunday mornings when I worship with other believers, the words I sing have new depth of meaning because I have experienced your presence throughout the week. Father, thank you that you alone are worthy of praise. Don't let me wander from this important truth, but continue to teach me how each moment of my life can be an act of worship.

Teach me your ways, O LORD, that I may live according to your truth! Grant me purity of heart, so that I may honor you. With all my heart I will praise you, O Lord my God. I will give glory to your name forever, for your love for me is very great. PSALM 86:11-13

☼ **A prayer about KNOWLEDGE**
How can I use my knowledge most effectively?

DEAR LORD,

Proverbs declares that reverence for you is the beginning of knowledge. Because you are omniscient—you have all knowledge—I can have complete confidence in the accuracy and authority of your Word. The more I learn about you, the more everything else makes sense. When I understand how strong and wise you are, my reverence for you grows by leaps and bounds.

Cry out for insight, and ask for understanding. Search for them. . . . Then you will understand what it means to fear the LORD, and you will gain knowledge of God.
PROVERBS 2:3-5

☼ **A prayer about AUTHENTICITY**
When I wonder if my faith is real

LORD,

If I want my faith to be truly genuine, I must ask the difficult question, "How pure are my motives?" Do I confess my sin because I've been caught, or because I am truly ashamed of what I've done? Are my good deeds because I want others to think well of me, or because I have genuine compassion for the needy? Lord, purify my heart.

Search me, O God, and know my heart; test me and know my anxious thoughts. PSALM 139:23

☼ A prayer about COMPROMISE
*When I need to find common ground without
compromising my convictions*

DEAR GOD,

I'm trying to reach an agreement, and I need the wisdom
to know when to compromise and when to stand firm
on my convictions. I have to be a student of your Word,
because it teaches me truth. And truth is where I must
draw the line, for to compromise your truth is to negotiate
with that which is unholy. Perhaps the test of acceptable
compromise is simpler than I realize: Can I reach a sat-
isfactory agreement without your truth being sacrificed?
To give up godliness for something less is a bad bargain.
So may I work for harmony and agreement whenever it is
possible, but when it is not, I pray that you would break
through the stalemate and make your will clear.

*Dear friend, don't let this bad example influence you. Follow
only what is good. Remember that those who do good prove
that they are God's children, and those who do evil prove
that they do not know God.* 3 JOHN 1:11

☼ **A prayer about WISDOM**
  When I need wisdom

DEAR LORD JESUS,

So often I know the facts, but I still don't know what to do about them. I need wisdom! Your Bible has so much to say about wisdom; in fact, the entire book of Proverbs is devoted to it. That's a good thing because life is messy, and getting through it gracefully requires much insight. I recognize that you, the all-powerful, all-knowing God, have designed this world in such a way that my choices really make a difference in the direction my life takes. So I need a lot of wisdom to make good choices. And you promise that you will supply plenty of wisdom to those who ask for it. Thank you for this essential gift. Wisdom begins with understanding that I am accountable to you, O Lord. Only your wisdom helps me develop a godly perspective that penetrates the deceptive and distorted messages of this world. I choose to apply your truth to my daily relationships and situations.

If you need wisdom, ask our generous God, and he will give it to you. He will not rebuke you for asking. JAMES 1:5

DAY 283

☀ **A prayer about BETRAYAL**
When a friend betrays me

JESUS,

I have been betrayed by my friend. Oh, how I want to retaliate. I want vengeance! Only through your power can I respond with love instead. Betrayal is an inevitable part of the human experience. Even you, dear Jesus, were betrayed. That doesn't make my betrayal any easier to accept, but it does help me gain perspective. Your response was to forgive your betrayers. Everything in me resists that! Please transform me so that I'm able to forgive, because that's the only healing for betrayal. No offense against me compares with my own offenses against you, Jesus, before you rescued me from sin. I am a forgiven person who must become a forgiving person. Only then will your power be revealed in me. I am here, and I am open to your transforming power.

"If your enemies are hungry, feed them. If they are thirsty, give them something to drink. In doing this, you will heap burning coals of shame on their heads." Don't let evil conquer you, but conquer evil by doing good.
ROMANS 12:20-21

⚙ **A prayer about DIFFERENCES**
When I'm feeling different

CHRIST JESUS,

Your Word tells me I am designed to contribute to the body of believers. Like the human body, the body of Christ is made up of separate and different parts, yet all parts work together to sustain life. Each believer has a unique role to play. My role will be different from others', but the beauty is that these differences help sustain your church and allow it to flourish. Lord Jesus, don't let me hold back because I desire another's gifts or because I think I have nothing to offer. Your Word tells me that I fit in and that I'm supposed to be unique. When I doubt I belong, encourage me through this thought so I will not abandon your body, the church, in this time of need.

He makes the whole body fit together perfectly. As each part does its own special work, it helps the other parts grow, so that the whole body is healthy and growing and full of love.
EPHESIANS 4:16

☼ A prayer about COMPARISON
When I need to resist comparing myself to others

GOD,

I'm constantly dwelling on one question: "How do I measure up?" This is one area where Satan has a foothold, and I know he is continually trying to convince me that my worth is based on how I compare to others in appearance, possessions, accomplishments, or social status. No wonder I constantly feel either inadequate and envious or full of pride. I'm tired of fighting this useless battle with myself. O God, I need to center my thoughts on your truth and your standards. Measured against your holiness, everyone falls short and is humbled; but in your eyes, every person is valued and loved—even me. I'm thankful that you never compare me with others, and because of that, neither should I. Help me to enjoy your grace, which has no comparison, and bask in the ways that you shower me with kindness and love. O God, my value is found in you alone.

Oh, that my actions would consistently reflect your decrees! Then I will not be ashamed when I compare my life with your commands. PSALM 119:5-6

❈ A prayer about SUCCESS
When I need to remember what success really is

DEAR LORD,

I want to be successful in your eyes. Help me always to measure success not by what I have, but by who I am; not by what I know, but by how I love; not by what I have achieved, but by the character I have built in others. May I always remember that partnering with you in this life is the best way to ensure true success.

Our goal is to please him. For we must all stand before Christ to be judged. We will each receive whatever we deserve for the good or evil we have done in this earthly body.
2 CORINTHIANS 5:9-10

DAY 287 *Prayerful Moment*

❈ A prayer about RISK
When I've been playing it safe

LORD,

Sometimes it seems that my faith centers on warnings to avoid things: the "thou shalt nots." But I long to do something positive for you—to take a faith adventure and learn to trust you more. I want to keep growing, and to do that, I need to leave behind my timidity and take a chance on you. Lord, give me the faith to risk everything for you.

Do not be afraid or discouraged, for the LORD will personally go ahead of you. He will be with you; he will neither fail you nor abandon you. DEUTERONOMY 31:8

☼ A prayer about ENEMIES
When I think about God's enemies

O LORD,

Today I pray that one of your enemies would become one of your followers! It is a mystery why you overwhelm some of your enemies, like the murderer Saul who became the apostle Paul, but seem to leave others alone. But almost every church around the world includes believers who once actively opposed you and your people. Your over-whelming love and grace flooded their souls, and now they bow before you as their Lord and King. So today, Lord, do that again, so that your mighty name might be glorified now and forever.

Saul was uttering threats with every breath and was eager to kill the Lord's followers. So he went to the high priest. He requested letters addressed to the synagogues in Damascus, asking for their cooperation in the arrest of any followers of the Way he found there. He wanted to bring them—both men and women—back to Jerusalem in chains. As he was approaching Damascus on this mission, a light from heaven suddenly shone down around him. He fell to the ground and heard a voice saying to him, "Saul! Saul! Why are you persecuting me?" "Who are you, lord?" Saul asked. And the voice replied, "I am Jesus, the one you are persecuting!"
ACTS 9:1-5

☼ **A prayer for GUIDANCE**
When I can't see God's plan for my life

DEAR GOD,

If I want to experience your guidance, I need to trust you. This means being confident that wherever I've been, wherever I am, and wherever I'm headed are all a part of your plan. It also means trusting your directions, even when I don't know the destination. If you were to show me too much of my future, I might become afraid of some hard times ahead or overconfident about my accomplishments. In either case, I might be tempted to stop trusting your wisdom for my life. Your guidance is like a flashlight that lights up just enough of the path ahead to show me where to take the next few steps. By guiding me step by step, Lord, you reveal your plan in your time. You unfold life's joys and sorrows in doses I can handle. Each day's circumstances then become proof that you have my best interests in mind. You have a definite plan for me. Help me to trust you to guide me each step of the way.

The LORD says, "I will guide you along the best pathway for your life. I will advise you and watch over you."
PSALM 32:8

☼ A prayer about INFLUENCE
When I feel discouraged about sharing my faith

DEAR JESUS,

Sometimes I get discouraged that I'm not leading others into a relationship with you. I try so hard to influence people, but sometimes the harder I try, the more they seem to pull away. Instead of focusing on the end results, please help me to focus on the process—living in daily obedience. That steady character and integrity is what will draw others to you, Jesus. On this side of eternity, I may not be able to see how my life influences others. But my job is to plant seeds of faith in the lives of people around me and trust that you will nourish those seeds until they grow into a saving relationship with you.

After all, who is Apollos? Who is Paul? We are only God's servants through whom you believed the Good News. Each of us did the work the Lord gave us. I planted the seed in your hearts, and Apollos watered it, but it was God who made it grow. It's not important who does the planting, or who does the watering. What's important is that God makes the seed grow. The one who plants and the one who waters work together with the same purpose. And both will be rewarded for their own hard work. I CORINTHIANS 3:5-8

☼ A prayer about LOVE
When I feel I need to earn God's love

GOD,

How freeing to know that your love is never something I can earn. It is a gift. If I compare my works to the deeds of those around me, I may feel I need to do more to be a better Christian. But obedience is not a prerequisite for your love. I obey you because I am already loved by you, not in order to be loved by you. Love and obedience become a refreshing cycle in our relationship. As I see you at work in my life every day, I am moved to greater obedience. The more I obey, the more joy I experience. Lord God, let the cycle continue today by showing me what small step of obedience I can take right now.

When you obey my commandments, you remain in my love. . . . I have told you these things so that you will be filled with my joy. Yes, your joy will overflow! JOHN 15:10-11

☼ A prayer for COMMUNICATION

*When I want to increase the lines of communication
with God*

DEAR LORD,

With all the means of communication I have at my fingertips—cell phone, Internet, e-mail—I am reminded about
the importance of communicating with you. But how
do I keep in touch with you? Sometimes I wish it were
as easy as calling you on the phone. If keeping in touch
is vital to the success of my interpersonal relationships,
it goes without saying that the same principle applies to
my relationship with you. What are the tools I need to
communicate with you? First, I can carve out more time
just to talk to you, and to listen. That's what I'm doing
now through prayer. Second, I can read your Word—your
book of communication to me. Third, I know that you
also speak to me through other people who are close to
you. I guess I do have lots of communication tools at my
fingertips. Lord, please show me how to better use them.
I want to stay in touch with you and experience a break-
through in my spiritual life.

*The LORD is close to all who call on him, yes, to all who call
on him in truth. . . . He hears their cries for help and rescues
them.* PSALM 145:18-19

☼ **A prayer for my CHURCH**
When I worship with other believers

GRACIOUS GOD,

How amazing that your Spirit lives in the heart of every believer, and that you are present in the community of the church. Participating with other believers in worship is so much more meaningful when I'm in the midst of it, actively involved. Father, thank you for the church. I pray that, as we gather this Sunday, you would fill us with the glory of your holy presence as we worship you together.

[Jesus said,] "Where two or three gather together as my followers, I am there among them." MATTHEW 18:20

DAY 294 *Prayerful Moment*

☼ **A prayer in SPIRITUAL DRYNESS**
When I have lost my enthusiasm for God

LORD,

I seldom feel passion anymore. I confess that I have allowed the challenges of life to drain my enthusiasm for you, and I have grown restless and weary on my spiritual journey. I don't want to just go through the motions, Lord. Show me the plans you have for me, and the simple ways I can serve you each day. Help me seize this very day to show your love to someone else.

You must warn each other every day, while it is still "today," so that none of you will be deceived by sin and hardened against God. HEBREWS 3:13

⚙ **A prayer for MIRACLES**
When I need a miracle

HOLY GOD,

The miracles recorded in the Bible can seem like ancient myths to those who fail to recognize your work in the world today. Back in the days of Moses, Pharaoh was blind to your power despite the miracles performed right before his eyes. I, too, can be blind to your miracles despite the mighty works you are doing all around me. It's impossible to see what I refuse to believe in. But when I cease doubting and allow myself to look for you, you show yourself in miraculous ways. I often expect a miracle to be a dramatic event, like someone being raised from the dead. But miracles are happening all around me! These supernatural occurrences may not be as dramatic as the parting of the Red Sea, but they are no less powerful. The birth of a baby, an awesome sunset, the healing of an illness, the restoration of a hopeless relationship, the rebirth of the earth in spring, salvation by faith alone—these are just a few incredible ways you act in your creation. When I think I need a miracle, remind me to look closer. They're happening all around me.

Come and see what our God has done, what awesome miracles he performs for people! PSALM 66:5

☼ A prayer about IMAGINATION
How can I use my imagination for God?

DEAR LORD,

Human imagination is a powerful thing. The tower of Babel was conceived out of pride, but the people's ability to design something so massive suggests there are few limits to what the human mind can imagine. My own imagination is powerful, and it can easily be hijacked by my sinful nature. Whatever controls my thoughts controls my imagination, too. When I'm stuck in a sinful cycle or controlled by a self-centered desire, my imagination easily concocts all kinds of dishonorable plans. O God, you have given me victory through Jesus Christ, so please don't let my mind be conquered by my sinful nature. Let my thoughts center on your ways so that your character will inspire my imagination. Keep my imagination from becoming a tool for destruction. Rather, let it be a tool for healthy innovation and vision!

Those who are dominated by the sinful nature think about sinful things, but those who are controlled by the Holy Spirit think about things that please the Spirit. So letting your sinful nature control your mind leads to death. But letting the Spirit control your mind leads to life and peace.
ROMANS 8:5-6

⚙ A prayer about **DISTRACTIONS**
When I feel sidetracked in serving God

GOD IN HEAVEN,

In many ways, I feel like my life is on hold right now. I feel so limited in my ministry for you. I had high hopes for all I would do for you, but then I wound up in a different place. Why, God? Why this situation that seems like a distraction from my true calling? You've reminded me about Paul and Silas when they were in prison. I would consider a jail sentence a definite distraction from my ability to serve you. Not Paul and Silas! Their location didn't keep them from their mission. They had been involved in a great ministry traveling around the world; now they were confined to a small room with a very small audience. But instead of pushing away the distraction, Paul and Silas embraced it, and you used them mightily! Sometimes being sidetracked seems as restricting as a jail cell. But God, maybe you want me to focus for a while on who and what is right in front of me. What I see as a distraction may actually be a calling from you to minister to new people in a new place. Lord, help me to let go of my expectations and to embrace this divine distraction.

Accept the way God does things, for who can straighten what he has made crooked? ECCLESIASTES 7:13

☀ A prayer about DISCONTENTMENT
When I'm never happy

O LORD,

Deep within my heart lurks a feeling of discontentment that is spreading. If I can't find a way to stop it, I'm afraid I'll wind up being disgruntled about everything. Every glass I look at seems half empty rather than half full, and I know this is affecting how I live. Through my disillusioned eyes, I don't have enough money, my spouse isn't the soul mate I'd dreamed of, my church isn't meeting my needs, my work is less than inspiring, and I can't do everything I want to do. Oh, where is this all taking me? I could ignore my feelings and just keep doing what I need to do, but that won't cure this restless attitude that is hounding me. Lord, I know this mind-set is dangerous because it causes me to focus on myself—what I don't have and what I'm not able to do. I need to change my thinking; that is the antidote. Please show me how. Transform my mind! Whenever I find myself thinking about what I don't have, help me to stop and take account of what I *do* have instead. I pray that I would keep my eyes on you and that you would show me how to serve those around me. If I take my eyes off myself, my discontentment may gradually turn into true satisfaction. Then, as I make you and others happy, I will find joy myself.

If you try to hang on to your life, you will lose it. But if you give up your life for my sake, you will save it.
MATTHEW 16:25

DAY 299

☼ **A prayer for ASSERTIVENESS**
When I need the courage to speak truth

LORD JESUS,

I am amazed at how assertive you often were when you spoke to the Pharisees. You stood up for what is right. May I have the courage to follow your example! Help me discern the difference between boldly speaking out for what is good, and bullying others into my way of thinking. Sometimes I am tempted to look the other way when others are making unethical choices or are behaving in offensive, inappropriate ways. I want to stand up for goodness and truth, while having the grace to confront lovingly. May my boldness be tempered with love, and may my convictions be reserved for upholding truth and justice, not for pursuing a personal agenda. The more I study your life, Lord Jesus, the better I will be at this.

I want you to insist on these teachings so that all who trust in God will devote themselves to doing good. TITUS 3:8

⚛ **A prayer about ADMIRATION**
   When I want to earn the respect of others

LORD,

Often I want others to respect me, so I emphasize my accomplishments. Still, I know that reflecting your love through faithful service is a more admirable quality. Open my eyes so that I may see others from your perspective, Lord. Soften my heart so I can love them as you do. And if others admire me, may it be because of your work in me.

There will be glory and honor and peace from God for all who do good. ROMANS 2:10

DAY 301 *Prayerful Moment*

⚛ **A prayer about TEMPTATION**
   When I need help to avoid temptation

LORD JESUS,

Temptation so often begins with my eyes. And how quickly it then travels to my heart. When I let my eyes linger where they shouldn't, before long I am being pulled in the wrong direction. I know that the first step in avoiding temptation is to avert my eyes. May I have the discipline to look away so I can avoid the tragic consequences of sin.

Late one afternoon, after his midday rest, David got out of bed and was walking on the roof of the palace. As he looked out over the city, he noticed a woman of unusual beauty taking a bath. He sent someone to find out who she was.
2 SAMUEL 11:2-3

☼ **A prayer about the PRESENCE OF GOD**
I can find God whenever I seek him

MIGHTY GOD,

One of your most mind-boggling characteristics is that you are omnipresent—everywhere at all times. I can't even begin to wrap my brain around this, but I find it reassuring. If you are everywhere at all times, then certainly you are with me now. And you promise that when I truly look for you, I will find you. God, I long to experience closeness with you. Thank you for giving me the ability to approach you anywhere through prayer. Thank you for giving me access to your thoughts and ways through your Word. Thank you that my life can be lived as worship to you in all times and places. Thank you that you are omnipresent and that I can draw closer to you. May I always be aware of your presence in new and wonderful ways.

I know the LORD is always with me. I will not be shaken, for he is right beside me. No wonder my heart is glad, and I rejoice. My body rests in safety. For you will not leave my soul among the dead or allow your holy one to rot in the grave. You will show me the way of life, granting me the joy of your presence and the pleasures of living with you forever.
PSALM 16:8-11

☼ A prayer for ENDURANCE
When I feel like giving up

DEAR JESUS,

Please grant me the endurance to finish well. I need your endurance to complete life's journey. When I get to the end, I'd love to have left a good reputation others can follow and a legacy of godly living. But the greatest reward for finishing well is the prize of eternal life with you. You have given this reward to all who have faith in you and who endure the challenges of the Christian life—persecution, ridicule, and temptation. Lord Jesus, please show me how to train myself so I can build up endurance for living a life of faith and staying strong to the end. May I not collapse during the race but find the strength to push on toward the goal of becoming more and more like you. Then, when I finally cross the finish line into your very presence, may I thank you for all the eternal rewards you have promised.

Since we are surrounded by such a huge crowd of witnesses to the life of faith, let us strip off every weight that slows us down, especially the sin that so easily trips us up. And let us run with endurance the race God has set before us. We do this by keeping our eyes on Jesus, the champion who initiates and perfects our faith. HEBREWS 12:1-2

☀ **A prayer in times of DOUBT**
When I doubt God can help me

O MIGHTY GOD,

Doubt can be a trapdoor to fear or a doorway to confident faith. I doubt you now, but I am choosing to trust you anyway. I believe that you are calling me to this task, so I am not surprised that the obstacles seem to be stacking up. I know this may be a test; you may be preparing to deepen my faith and strengthen my character so that I will know it is really you—rather than my own efforts—coming to my rescue. As the obstacles pile up, I realize I am no longer in charge. Only you can help me now; I can't accomplish the job on my own. I am ready to give you the credit rather than take it for myself. I don't want my doubts to lead me to fear, Lord. Please help me to be courageous and to hold on to my belief that you have called me to do something for you. Oh, that I would see your work and know that you are my God.

Don't be afraid, for I am with you. Don't be discouraged, for I am your God. I will strengthen you and help you. I will hold you up with my victorious right hand. ISAIAH 41:10

☼ **A prayer about APOLOGY**
When I'm having trouble accepting an apology

LORD JESUS,

Someone who has wronged me has apologized. But rather than accepting her apology, I want to punish her further by lashing out in anger or making her suffer just a little bit more. I know that's not right. When you walked this earth as a man, you forgave unconditionally, even those who plotted to kill you. Please fill my heart with that kind of unconditional love, which will lead to the complete forgiveness you exemplified. Help me to see that true forgiveness is not grudging or sparing but generous, joyful, and healing. When I accept an apology in this way, it brings healing to my soul. It also creates a divine moment in my friend's life because she gets to see the same kind of mercy you show me when you forgive my sin. Dear Jesus, may that kind of forgiveness start with me and change the world.

[The son] returned home to his father. And while he was still a long way off, his father saw him coming. Filled with love and compassion, he ran to his son, embraced him, and kissed him. LUKE 15:20

☼ A prayer about FEARING GOD
When I need more of the fear of God

ALMIGHTY GOD,

Fearing you is not the same as being afraid of you. If I were afraid of you, I would stay away. But fearing you means being awed by your power and goodness, and that draws me closer to you and the blessings you provide. Perhaps the fear I have for you is like the respect I might have for a beloved teacher, coach, parent, or mentor. My respect motivates me to do my best and to avoid doing anything that would hurt you. May I fear you because of your awesome power, and love you because you have used that power to rescue me from sin. What could be more amazing? I fully recognize that I don't deserve it. But how I rejoice that instead of punishing me, you shower me with mercy and forgiveness. May that kind of fear draw me into the security of your loving arms day after day.

How joyful are those who fear the LORD—all who follow his ways! PSALM 128:1

☼ A prayer about PRIORITIES
When life feels too busy to make time for God

DEAR GOD,

My priorities are often in the wrong order. Some days my life seems to skip from one urgent interruption to another. I am so easily distracted and often confuse what is urgent with what's important. But when I put you first, Lord, you give me the proper perspective and help me put everything else in its rightful place. Lord, show me where my focus should be today.

Seek the Kingdom of God above all else, and live righteously, and he will give you everything you need. MATTHEW 6:33

DAY 308 *Prayerful Moment*

☼ A prayer of BROKENNESS
When I've hit the bottom

O GOD,

Please turn my brokenness into a divine encounter with you. I feel overwhelmed by my circumstances, and I know that the only way out is through your help. I feel as if I've hit rock bottom, and I realize, Lord, how utterly dependent I am on you. I cannot take another step without you. Make this a turning point for me. I release my future into your loving hands. Draw close to me in my brokenness and restore my fellowship with you.

The LORD is close to the brokenhearted; he rescues those whose spirits are crushed. PSALM 34:18

☼ **A prayer for PEACE**
When I struggle to experience God's peace

HEAVENLY FATHER,

When I allow myself to trust that you are always watching over me, peace settles in my heart, even in the midst of difficult circumstances. This sounds so simple, but it is a step of faith for me. I have experienced your peace in troubled times, so I know that peace will not prevent me from encountering difficulties. However, it will give me the final victory over them. You promise to give me eternal life in heaven if I accept your free gift of salvation, you promise that Satan cannot take this gift away, and you promise to give me peace of mind and heart. Because these promises come from your eternal Word, I have total confidence in them. I praise you because no matter what happens, you will allow me to experience the inner peace that comes from knowing I am in your care.

I am leaving you with a gift—peace of mind and heart. And the peace I give is a gift the world cannot give. So don't be troubled or afraid. JOHN 14:27

☀ **A prayer for DISCIPLINE**
When I need a heart more open to God's discipline

O MERCIFUL FATHER,

Like the people of Jerusalem in the days of the biblical prophets, I can stubbornly refuse to listen to you—or to anyone else—and ignore the correction that could help me. I don't want to be like that! Please don't let me rebel against you, O God. If I do, you may use adversity to get my reluctant attention. If discipline is necessary, help me to submit to it; for without your loving hand of correction, I could continue to stray until I no longer even hear your voice. May I always stay open to your discipline because I know it is done in love and not anger, in mercy and not vengeance. Be gentle, Lord, I pray, and grow in me a teachable, malleable heart that will eagerly learn from you.

Joyful are those you discipline, LORD, those you teach with your instructions. PSALM 94:12

☼ **A prayer about the PAST**
When I'm feeling regret about my past

DEAR GOD,

I've had some wonderful moments in life, but I've also had times that I regret. I know that the way I view the past affects how I live today, so I want to deal with it correctly. The apostle Paul's example always encourages me. Though he became one of the great leaders of the early church, he had a past he wished he could forget. What an immense burden of regret he could have carried. But Paul understood that his past had been redeemed through the blood of Christ, and he was able to move forward in service to you. What an example! Lord, I pray for those who have a strong spiritual heritage. I pray they would not take their legacy for granted but would pour into others the love that was poured into them. I pray also for those whose past is filled with regret. Show them that you are always ready to forgive us, to cleanse us on the inside, and give us a fresh start. I pray for those who have been victims of abuse, neglect, or violence. May they know that they are valued, loved, and cherished by you and that you want to redeem them. You are a God who longs to restore us. Please remove the guilt, regret, and shame of my past and free me to live in peace with purpose and joy.

I focus on this one thing: Forgetting the past and looking forward to what lies ahead, I press on to reach the end of the race and receive the heavenly prize for which God, through Christ Jesus, is calling us. PHILIPPIANS 3:13-14

☼ **A prayer about being an EXAMPLE**
  When I want to set a godly example for those I love

DEAR LOVING FATHER,

If my children watched my life, what would they conclude about the importance of my relationship with you? As I strive to be a good example for others, including my own children, may I remember you first thing in the morning and fall asleep with you on my mind. May I remember you as the source of hope when I think I've lost all hope. May I remember you with a thankful heart when I have plenty and when I have little. May I meditate on your great love for me throughout each day. May I speak of your love and grace in front of others. And Lord, may I weave you into the fabric of my life so that my children and grandchildren will be encouraged from their earliest days to love you with all their hearts.

You must love the LORD your God with all your heart, all your soul, and all your strength. And you must commit your-selves wholeheartedly to these commands that I am giving you today. Repeat them again and again to your children. Talk about them when you are at home and when you are on the road, when you are going to bed and when you are getting up. Tie them to your hands and wear them on your forehead as reminders. Write them on the doorposts of your house and on your gates. DEUTERONOMY 6:5-9

☼ A prayer about LIMITATIONS
When I don't want my limitations to hold me back

GOD ALMIGHTY,

With each passing year I become more aware of my limitations. It's not just physical limitations but emotional ones that leave me feeling drained and empty. But in your great wisdom, you allow every person to have weaknesses—not to discourage us, but to help us realize our utter need for you. For it is in weakness that your strength shines. And so, O Lord, I ask that your strength would overcome my limitations. May I be able to accomplish something great despite my weakness, and may it be obvious to those watching that you are working through me. Then you will receive the credit and be glorified. Jesus said, "What is impossible for people is possible with God" (Luke 18:27). Oh, may it be so as you work your mighty power through me. May my limitations not discourage but rather encourage me, because they show I am ready for your power to be unleashed in my life. God, I praise you that I don't have to be more than I am for you to do great things in me.

Each time [the Lord] said, "My grace is all you need. My power works best in weakness." So now I am glad to boast about my weaknesses, so that the power of Christ can work through me. 2 CORINTHIANS 12:9

⚙ A prayer about PLEASURE
When I delight in doing what God commands

DEAR GOD,

My heart is deeply satisfied when I delight in doing what brings you joy. I know you always desire what is best for those who trust in you. Therefore it gives me great joy to follow you faithfully. Thank you that finding pleasure in obedience is the key to enjoying life as you intended—to the fullest!

How I delight in your commands! How I love them!
PSALM 119:47

DAY 315 *Prayerful Moment*

⚙ A prayer for AFFIRMATION
When I seek assurance from God

LORD,

I find assurance in knowing that you created me to be in fellowship with you. You ransomed me from the pit, even to the point of sacrificing your own Son to die for all people. Lord, I want to be all that you created me to be. Help me to realize where I have believed the lies of the world that lure me to seek my worth in unworthy things. I long to realize how fully you love and value me, O God.

We know how dearly God loves us, because he has given us the Holy Spirit to fill our hearts with his love. ROMANS 5:5

☀ **A prayer about PAIN**
When I need to see some hope in the pain

DEAR JESUS,

Sometimes it's hard to see you in the pain of the present. I realize that trusting you does not produce a storybook life in which every problem is quickly resolved. Sometimes people get sick and don't get better; relationships break down and can't be restored; jobs are lost. How I thank you, however, that not only are you with me in my pain, but I am assured of a happy ending where pain will disappear forever. When you return, discomfort, disappointment, disease, pain, and death will be gone, and I will live with joy in your presence forever. I praise you, Lord Jesus! Because this happy ending is utterly certain, I can endure the unanswered questions and unending crises of this life. How I thank you for the gift of hope in the present pain.

God himself will be with them. He will wipe every tear from their eyes, and there will be no more death or sorrow or crying or pain. All these things are gone forever.
REVELATION 21:3-4

☀ **A prayer for HUMILITY**
When pride might be getting the best of me

DEAR GOD,

Please show me what it means to be humble. Then perhaps I will be able to find the delicate balance between recognizing my sinful flaws and knowing how much you value me. I know pride is wrong because it elevates me above others, and often above you. Oh, don't let me think I am the only one who knows what's going on and what is best. On the other hand, degrading myself is also unacceptable because it denies the value you have placed upon me. I am called your child! You created me in your image and sent your Son to die for me; therefore, I have great value in your eyes. Lord, I guess true humility involves seeing myself as you see me: a person with flaws and a sinful nature, no better or worse in your sight than anyone else—but a person who is worth dying for. No wonder true humility is the pathway to discovering how to serve you and other people.

Pride leads to disgrace, but with humility comes wisdom.
PROVERBS 11:2

☼ A prayer for the IMPOSSIBLE
Can God do the impossible for me?

ALMIGHTY GOD,

Your Word is filled with stories of the impossible: a flood covers the earth; a sea is parted so people can walk through it; the sun keeps shining until a battle can be won; a man survives three days in the belly of a fish; a virgin gives birth to a baby boy. To the person who does not believe in you, these stories defy logic. But those who believe you are the Creator of all things also believe that you can alter what you created; you can break natural law to cause something supernatural to happen. It takes eyes of faith to believe the impossible. When my faith is strong, Lord, I understand that what I see is not all there is. I recognize the "impossible" things you do for your people because I believe that anything is possible for you. Dear God, please teach me to recognize the impossible things you accomplish for me and around me each day: the gift of forgiveness; the change of seasons; the intricacies of the human body and its ability to heal; the exact conditions needed to support life on this earth; the birth of a baby. The more I see you accomplish the impossible, the stronger my faith grows. You specialize in doing what, from a human perspective, is impossible. But the end of my abilities is the beginning of yours. I believe you can do the impossible for me.

[Jesus] replied, "What is impossible for people is possible with God." LUKE 18:27

⚙ **A prayer for COMFORT**
*When I need God to speak comfort to me in
difficult times*

ALMIGHTY GOD,

I'm amazed at how my need for comfort and your supply
of comfort are always in perfect balance. You welcome me
to call on you in my distress because that demonstrates my
trust in you. When I'm lonely, troubled, or afraid, I can
cry out and know you will answer. The Bible tells me that
you love to show your power through my weakness. You
are my source of comfort, and the greatest resource for
finding that comfort is your Word. Your promises encourage me and give me confident assurance that I will one day
live forever in peace and security with you. Your Word is as
close as my fingertips, and your presence is as close as my
whispered prayer. Thank you that there is no one closer to
me than you.

*Every word of God proves true. He is a shield to all who
come to him for protection.* PROVERBS 30:5

☀ A prayer about DISAPPOINTMENT
When I feel constantly disappointed

O FATHER,

I deal with disappointment in some form almost every day, and I must come to grips with this issue in my heart. Disappointment sometimes comes because I don't feel "good enough." It also comes because I expect too much of myself and others. When I don't meet my own expectations, I wallow in regret and self-doubt. When others don't meet my expectations, I'm quick to blame them and shame them. Disappointment carries some heavy baggage: discouragement, depression, anger, bitterness, and shame. O God, I need your help to break this cycle. Why am I trying to be perfect when only you are perfect? Why do I expect others to meet my needs when you are the only one who can truly be everything to me? Father, help me to stop dreaming about what could be and start focusing on what is truth—what is real in the here and now. Help me to be thankful for what I have instead of always expecting more. O God, next time I'm tempted to place unrealistic expectations on myself, may I ask, "Lord, what do *you* expect of me?" When I expect others to satisfy all my needs, may I turn to you say, "Lord, you know my needs, and you are everything to me." Lord God, may you begin this most important change in my heart today.

This hope will not lead to disappointment. For we know how dearly God loves us, because he has given us the Holy Spirit to fill our hearts with his love. ROMANS 5:5

☼ A prayer for ENERGY
When I'm burdened by my past

DEAR JESUS,

I know I am supposed to let go of the past and move on, but sometimes I realize I'm still carrying burdens from long ago. When this happens, I feel heavyhearted and drained. The more I drag forward from yesterday, the heavier the load I will carry today and the less energy I will have for tomorrow. Please free me from the past so I can channel my energy into making today all you want it to be.

Dear brothers and sisters, . . . I focus on this one thing: Forgetting the past and looking forward to what lies ahead. PHILIPPIANS 3:13

DAY 322 *Prayerful Moment*

☼ A prayer of DISCOURAGEMENT
When I start to feel like the victim

LORD,

Sometimes when I'm discouraged, I start to feel sorry for myself. I become so focused on my own concerns I forget that others are suffering too—and many far worse than I. Forgive my selfish nature and give me a heart of compassion. Show me how to be a comfort to others in their struggles.

Be strong in your faith. Remember that your Christian brothers and sisters all over the world are going through the same kind of suffering you are. 1 PETER 5:8-9

☼ **A prayer for TENDERNESS**
When I want to feel more compassion for others

DEAR GOD,

I long to regain some tenderness in my heart, and I know that tenderness starts with you. It is amazing that you, the God of the universe, care for me with compassion. Experiencing gentle, merciful love from your hand softens my heart to feel for the needs of others. You replace my bitter heart, hardened and dulled by years of sin and hurt, with a soft and tender heart. You plant a compassionate spirit within me! Thank you, Lord. Now that I have your tenderhearted nature within me, let me realize the depth of your love for me as I care for others. Where before my heart was unfeeling, let me now be overwhelmed with a compassion born out of my own gratitude for all you have done for me.

[God said,] "I will sprinkle clean water on you, and you will be clean. Your filth will be washed away, and you will no longer worship idols. And I will give you a new heart, and I will put a new spirit in you. I will take out your stony, stubborn heart and give you a tender, responsive heart. And I will put my Spirit in you so that you will follow my decrees and be careful to obey my regulations."

EZEKIEL 36:25-27

☼ A prayer about WARNINGS
When some of the Bible's rules frustrate me

O GOD,

When you warn me about something, please help me to be grateful and not resentful. I'm grateful for red lights at intersections warning me to stop. I'm grateful for a poison label warning me to keep a bottle of cleanser out of my children's reach. I'm grateful for an ambulance siren warning me to get out of the way. Lord, I know these kinds of warnings are good for me. Please help me to keep the right perspective about your warnings too. When the Bible tells me to watch out for certain things that could hurt me, help me to listen! I don't want to view your warnings as intrusions that prevent me from enjoying life, but rather as blessings that protect me so I can enjoy life more. Your guidelines will save me from the consequences of foolish actions. Your warning to avoid sexual immorality, for example, prevents me from the tragedy of a broken heart or the regret of betrayal. O Lord, help me not to rebel against the very things that are designed to protect me. Let me see your warnings as merciful acts that allow me to enjoy real joy and freedom.

The laws of the LORD are true; each one is fair. They are more desirable than gold, even the finest gold. They are sweeter than honey, even honey dripping from the comb. They are a warning to your servant, a great reward for those who obey them. PSALM 19:9-11

DAY 325

☀ A prayer about BLESSINGS
When I need perspective on God's blessings

LORD GOD,

The greatest blessings you have given me are far more valuable than money or possessions. These are blessings that keep giving: joy, peace of heart, spiritual gifts, family, friendships, and the confidence of eternal life. You have given me far more than I deserve, and you give it freely simply because you love me. I could never earn the blessings that come from walking in your presence, so my obedience is not rooted in pride. No, I obey you because I am deeply grateful for all of these undeserved gifts. I enjoy them all the more knowing there are no strings attached. Thank you, Lord. May my heart always be humble and thankful to you.

He does not punish us for all our sins; he does not deal harshly with us, as we deserve. For his unfailing love toward those who fear him is as great as the height of the heavens above the earth. PSALM 103:10-11

☼ **A prayer about CHURCH**
When I need affirmation that church is important

LORD GOD,

Thank you for my church. I need to be reminded that together all believers make up your family, and it is only by meeting together that we can learn to lean on each other. I am grateful that the church equips me to do your work and encourages me in my faith. As I am involved with my church, Lord, let me learn to work in unity with other believers, reconciling differences in a way that is only possible through your Spirit. As we meet together, may we build each other up and help each other. Thank you that every believer is important; your body is not complete unless each of us is part of it. I know you are present everywhere, Lord, but you are present in a special way when believers gather to worship you, serve you, and learn about you. Help me look forward to church this week.

Let us not neglect our meeting together, as some people do, but encourage one another, especially now that the day of his return is drawing near. HEBREWS 10:25

☼ A prayer about CHANGE
When I need to deal with all the change in my life

GOOD AND GRACIOUS GOD,

I'll state the obvious: change is stressful! I know that change is one of the great constants of life, but that doesn't make it any easier. Whether big or little, change keeps coming at me. People change, relationships change, jobs change. I know some changes are positive—thank you for those! Other changes seem negative, and I need to learn to thank you for those as well. I'm grateful that you promise to redeem even the most difficult things that can happen to me. And I thank you that when I go through traumatic change, I am reminded that you are changeless and dependable. Father, there is one big change you ask from me, and that is an inner change of heart called repentance. Please work out this radical transformation in my heart so that the trajectory of my life will be positively changed forever.

I will give you a new heart, and I will put a new spirit in you. I will take out your stony, stubborn heart and give you a tender, responsive heart. EZEKIEL 36:26

☼ **A prayer about APPRECIATION**
What is the importance of expressing my appreciation to others?

LORD JESUS,

Sometimes it's just nice to feel appreciated. So why am I so reluctant to offer that gift to others? Don't let me miss an opportunity to express my appreciation—to thank people and build them up. People need to know that they're noticed, cared for, and important. Work through me, Lord, so that my words of encouragement may bring a spark of divine grace into someone else's life.

I have not stopped thanking God for you. I pray for you constantly. EPHESIANS 1:16

DAY 329 *Prayerful Moment*

☼ **A prayer for PROVISION**
When I wonder if God will meet my needs

DEAR FATHER,

You've promised to meet my needs, but too often I confuse my desires with my real needs. You haven't promised me material wealth, but you have promised to develop in me the qualities that reflect your nature. Better yet, you have promised to preserve my soul for all eternity. Thank you, Father, for caring for me as only you can.

This same God who takes care of me will supply all your needs from his glorious riches, which have been given to us in Christ Jesus. PHILIPPIANS 4:19

⚙ **A prayer for THANKFULNESS**
How can I thank God when life is difficult?

DEAR GOD,

In the middle of difficult circumstances, I continue to be thankful to you. I know the difficulties in my life come for many reasons. I may be experiencing the consequences of my own sin, I may be suffering because of someone else's sin, or I may be caught in unfortunate circumstances that are really no one's fault. Whatever the case, may I be thankful that you redeem my mistakes, teach me wisdom through adversity, promise to help me through the tough times, and guarantee me eternal life that is forever free from suffering. A God who redeems all troubles is a God worthy of praise and thanksgiving. I praise you, Lord!

Joseph replied [to his brothers], "Don't be afraid of me. . . . You intended to harm me, but God intended it all for good. He brought me to this position so I could save the lives of many people." GENESIS 50:19-20

☀ A prayer of BROKENNESS
When I am broken

O MERCIFUL GOD,

I am broken. I have fallen into sin, and now I fall to my knees before you. I am not going to run from you; no, I am staying right here at your feet, for I desperately need your mercy. I am reminded that King David committed adultery with Bathsheba and then had her husband murdered—it doesn't get much worse than that! Yet when he was confronted with his sin, David didn't run from you. He didn't make excuses for his failure, nor did he give up in despair. Instead, he acknowledged your justice and cast himself on your mercy. Now I am doing the same. I confess my sin to you and acknowledge my full dependence upon you. I cast myself on your mercy and ask you to rescue and restore me. I know the way back will be long and hard, but I also know that my redemption will be a victory for you. May your power shine through my weakness so that you, O God, will be praised.

Have mercy on me, O God, because of your unfailing love. Because of your great compassion, blot out the stain of my sins. Wash me clean from my guilt. Purify me from my sin. For I recognize my rebellion; it haunts me day and night.
PSALM 51:1-3

⚙ **A prayer for GRACE**
When I understand God's grace, I will be gracious with others

O GOD,

I have experienced your grace as both a onetime act (your undeserved favor giving me salvation through faith in Jesus) and as a way of life (your ongoing work within me). Grace is your special favor. When I think about how your mercy has changed my life, I am so humbled. Because of your grace, you give me blessings I don't deserve, and in your mercy, you withhold the punishment my sins do deserve. Let my personal experience with your tender-hearted mercy translate into heartfelt acceptance of others. I pray that you would increase my understanding of your grace so I will be moved to share that same freedom with those around me. Don't let me stop with one act of kindness, but help me to remember that your grace is an ongoing work in my life. Please develop a spirit of graciousness and mercy in me that consistently spills into the lives of others, so they, too, might be blessed by your special favor.

God saved you by his grace when you believed. And you can't take credit for this; it is a gift from God. Salvation is not a reward for the good things we have done, so none of us can boast about it. EPHESIANS 2:8-9

DAY 333

☼ **A prayer for STRENGTH**
*When I want to experience more of God's strength
in my life*

O GOD OF HEAVEN,

How I long for more spiritual strength. I desire the faith to move mountains, the power to lift burdens, a foundation deep enough to hold up against the forces of temptation, and the confident security of eternal salvation. How do I get this kind of strength? First, help me recognize that the power you used to raise Jesus from the dead is available to me now so I can live more effectively and courageously for you. Next, Lord, please help me realize that you promise to give me inner strength through the power of your own Holy Spirit when I depend on you and trust you to do what is best for me. Finally, may I remember that your power works best through my weaknesses. Where I am weak and limited, you promise to supply the strength to help me overcome great obstacles. How grateful I am that you love to work through my weaknesses, because then everyone can see that it is you, not me, supplying the strength. Then I will be a testimony to the reality of God living in me. And you will be praised.

The eyes of the LORD search the whole earth in order to strengthen those whose hearts are fully committed to him.
2 CHRONICLES 16:9

⚙ **A prayer for PURPOSE**
*When I wonder if God has a specific purpose for
my life*

DEAR LORD,

I want my life to have purpose. According to your Word,
I must let you transform my very thinking—and then I
will know your will for me. In a general sense, I know my
purpose is to let your love shine through me to make an
impact on others. But in a specific sense, I know you want
me to use my spiritual gifts to serve you within my sphere
of influence. Could it be that the more I fulfill my general
purpose, the clearer my specific calling will become? May
my ultimate goal in life be to reach not the places I desire
but the destinations you want for me. As I passionately
pursue the purpose you have assigned for me, you promise
to give my life greater meaning, lasting significance, and
eternal results. May it be so, Lord.

*Let God transform you into a new person by changing the way
you think. Then you will learn to know God's will for you,
which is good and pleasing and perfect.* ROMANS 12:2

✺ **A prayer of FAITHFULNESS**
God is so faithful to me

DEAR GOD,

I praise you because you are faithful. You always do what you say you will do. Your record is flawless; your Word is eternal and true. I know I can count on you to fulfill all your promises for the future. Even more, I have seen your faithfulness in answered prayer, timely provision, gentle discipline, and encouraging blessings. Thank you, Lord.

You can be sure of this: The LORD set apart the godly for himself. The LORD will answer when I call to him.
PSALM 4:3

DAY 336 *Prayerful Moment*

✺ **A prayer about CHALLENGES**
When I face a great challenge

LORD GOD,

Often it seems that those who possess great faith are risk-takers who embrace life's challenges. Abram left everything he knew when he responded to your challenge to move to a new place. And Moses, though initially reluctant, stood before Pharaoh and demanded the release of the Israelites. I see that great things do not happen without challenges. So, Lord, the next time I am faced with a challenge, empower me to step out boldly in obedience to you.

In your strength I can crush an army; with my God I can scale any wall. 2 SAMUEL 22:30

☼ A prayer about INJUSTICE
When I long for justice

O LORD,

There is such injustice in the world. I see it everywhere—government, business, communities, even families! Why are we so prone to treat our fellow human beings unjustly? How might I be contributing to this plague of injustice? I admit that sometimes I get angry at you for allowing such injustice in the world. But then I remember that you did not create it. Injustice happens because you created people with free will. We can choose good or evil, right or wrong. Without that freedom, we would only be puppets of a divine dictator, not people who can choose to love and do what is right. To think that the existence of injustice means that you condone it is contrary to your righteous nature and what the Bible teaches about sin. Help me admit that injustice is humans' fault, and I have a part in it. Now help me be part of the solution. Give me the opportunity and the courage, Lord, to speak up against injustice when I see it, and to do something—*anything*—to bring justice to someone who needs it. Help me do my part to rescue those in need, and may others do their part as well. Father, I look forward to that day when you promise that justice will rule in every corner of people's hearts throughout the whole earth.

Those who plant injustice will harvest disaster, and their reign of terror will come to an end. PROVERBS 22:8

☼ **A prayer in times of LONELINESS**
When my relationships with others fail or disappoint

LORD,

Even when I feel alone, you are always with me. The Bible tells me you are thinking about me all the time, and I'm so grateful for that. But when I am abandoned or betrayed by others, I want to throw up my hands and give up. I know I shouldn't abandon all relationships because a few have failed or disappointed. Lord, even though I feel lonely, I don't want to start feeling discouraged or sorry for myself. That just isolates me from you and from any hope of genuine relationship. Please use this "alone time" to show me your faithfulness. As I see your faithful presence and abundant mercy, may I be compelled to reach out to others. Keep me from becoming self-focused; help me instead to focus on serving others and caring for their needs. Lord, I long for genuine friendship, and I ask that you would bring godly relationships into my life. But until then and always, I am grateful for your faithful presence with me.

How precious are your thoughts about me, O God. They cannot be numbered! PSALM 139:17

☼ **A prayer about BEAUTY**
When I want to display God's beauty in all seasons
of life

HEAVENLY FATHER,

Things are loveliest and best when they are blooming in the right season. Life has many seasons, each with its own beauty. How can I bloom in every season? By following you and reflecting the beauty of your holiness, love, and wisdom. Father, the Bible says that you are the great gardener. Apart from you, I will wither and die. O Lord, I give myself to you and ask that you would prune away the useless and rotten parts of my heart so I will bloom in your love through all the seasons of life.

Oh, the joys of those who do not follow the advice of the wicked, or stand around with sinners, or join in with mockers. But they delight in the law of the LORD, meditating on it day and night. They are like trees planted along the riverbank, bearing fruit each season. Their leaves never wither, and they prosper in all they do. PSALM 1:1-3

☼ **A prayer about CHILDREN**
When I want to teach my children about God

HEAVENLY FATHER,

I want to teach my children about you, but I need your help. I'm so tired most of the time that I fear I miss out on teachable moments. O Lord, please supply me with the energy to respond to my children's natural curiosity about you. When my child asks about a tree or a caterpillar, help me to explain how any creation is a gift from you. You commanded the Israelites to set up a memorial that would attract children's curiosity and create teaching moments for the Israelite parents. Please show me how I can start conversations about you with my children by setting up reminders of you in my home. May these reminders give me chances to share the great things you have done. Don't let me miss these most important opportunities! The next time my child asks me to tell a story, bring to my mind a story from the Bible or from my own spiritual journey. I want my children to know that you are real and loving and enjoy being a part of their lives.

[Moses said,] "Commit yourselves wholeheartedly to these words of mine. Tie them to your hands and wear them on your forehead as reminders. Teach them to your children. Talk about them when you are at home and when you are on the road, when you are going to bed and when you are getting up." DEUTERONOMY 11:18-19

DAY 341

☼ **A prayer for my NEIGHBORS**
When I want to reach out to others

DEAR JESUS,

I tend to think of my neighbors as the people who live next door or across the street. But your teachings expand my neighborhood to involve anyone around me who needs your love and care. This means that the people next to me on a plane, my coworkers, or the homeless in my town are also my neighbors. Not only that, but my neighborhood really should expand to people around the world who need your love. Teach me to think about the people I meet or hear about as my neighbors so I can treat them as you would if you were still walking on this earth. Jesus, what neighbors will come across my path today? Don't let me miss these encounters as divine moments that allow me to share your love.

"Now which of these three would you say was a neighbor to the man who was attacked by bandits?" Jesus asked. The man replied, "The one who showed him mercy." Then Jesus said, "Yes, now go and do the same." LUKE 10:36-37

☼ **A prayer for FAMILY**
How can my family make a difference for God?

LORD,

How can my family be influential for you? I pray for each member and for my family as a whole. I ask that you would use us to accomplish great things for your kingdom. With grace and truth, let us profoundly affect the lives of people around us.

How joyful are those who fear the LORD and delight in obeying his commands. Their children will be successful everywhere; an entire generation of godly people will be blessed. PSALM 112:1, 2

DAY 343 *Prayerful Moment*

☼ **A prayer for ADVICE**
When I need godly advice

HEAVENLY FATHER,

Why do I sometimes look for godly advice from people who aren't close to you? No wonder their counsel doesn't seem to help! When I'm looking for godly advice, please lead me to people who are committed to telling the truth, even if it's what I don't want to hear. Lead me to people who are close to you, who know your Word and can wisely discern what is right. Lord, please give me the desire to always seek godly counsel.

The godly offer good counsel; they teach right from wrong.
PSALM 37:30

⚙ A prayer about SERVICE
When I need some motivation to serve

DEAR JESUS,

You say that you came to earth to be a servant. May that be my goal as well. Perhaps you place such a high value on serving because it is centered on others rather than on myself, which is the essence of effective Christian living. Lord Jesus, I want to serve. Please transform my simple acts of service into something profound and purposeful. May my singing join a profound chorus of praise that ministers to an entire congregation. May my tithing turn into a profound act of mercy that touches the heart of the needy person who benefits from it. May my teaching Sunday school turn into a profound moment in the heart of a child who suddenly realizes her need for salvation. And may my simple act of visiting shut-ins turn into a profound moment of encouragement. Jesus, I pray for boldness to step out in faith to serve others. I will trust you to turn even my simple acts into meaningful works for your Kingdom.

Among you it will be different. Whoever wants to be a leader among you must be your servant. . . . For even the Son of Man came not to be served but to serve others and to give his life as a ransom for many. MATTHEW 20:26, 28

☼ **A prayer about SHARING**
When I want it all for myself

LORD GOD,

Why do I find it so hard to share? Why do I struggle to relinquish my possessions and give of myself to others? At the core of my nature is the desire to get, not to give. When I read your Word, I know in my heart that this self-serving desire is wrong. I often feel convicted to share many things: my resources, faith, love, time, talents, money, and possessions. At times I have experienced the enjoyment of sharing with others the blessings you have given me. Lord, you have shared so many of your great riches with me. You have blessed me with special gifts. You even gave your Son, Jesus, to pay the price for my sins. How generous you have been with me. I ask you to help me remove the self-serving attitudes that keep me closed off to others. Teach me by your generous spirit to live with open hands.

May you be filled with joy, always thanking the Father. He has enabled you to share in the inheritance that belongs to his people, who live in the light. COLOSSIANS 1:11-12

☀ A prayer about MYSTERY
  When I wonder about the ambiguities of my faith

ALMIGHTY GOD,

How I praise you that you always act justly and rightly. Your truth never changes, so I can count on you to keep your Word. And yet I also praise you for moving in unpredictable and mysterious ways. Your plans sometimes defy human logic—and for good reason. If I could know you completely, if I could predict your every move, then I would be equal to you. I don't need a God who is my equal; I need to worship a God who is far beyond my capabilities in every way. Your mysterious aspects teach me to respect you and show you the reverence you deserve. Thank you that the Christian life involves continually learning spiritual truths about you as your Spirit reveals them. May I be open to going wherever you lead, while trusting that your perfect character will always stay the same. Only you, O Lord, are worthy of my praise and worship.

How great is our Lord! His power is absolute! His understanding is beyond comprehension! . . . Can you solve the mysteries of God? Can you discover everything about the Almighty? PSALM 147:5; JOB 11:7

☼ A prayer for PERSEVERANCE
*When I need the perseverance to get through
tough times*

DEAR LORD,

In the middle of my problems I often want to give up.
How do I see my way through to the end? I need more
perseverance. I have heard perseverance defined as "courage stretched out." I guess that means that although you
sometimes deliver your people out of difficult or painful circumstances, you often call us to faithfulness in the
midst of trials. And according to your Word, perseverance
is not just enduring difficult situations; it is overcoming
them with obedience, hope, and joy. If I don't learn to
persevere through my struggles, I will fall into the habit of
giving up. Please help me, Lord, to persevere until I come
out on the other side. Doing that will strengthen my faith.
Then I will more clearly see the benefits of obeying you,
and I will develop confidence that when problems come
again, I will get through them with your help.

*We think you ought to know, dear brothers and sisters, about
the trouble we went through in the province of Asia. We
were crushed and overwhelmed beyond our ability to endure,
and we thought we would never live through it. In fact, we
expected to die. But as a result, we stopped relying on ourselves and learned to rely only on God, who raises the dead.*
2 CORINTHIANS 1:8-9

⚙ **A prayer about the PROMISES OF GOD**
*When I wonder if God's promises in the Bible apply
to me today*

LORD GOD,

Sometimes I feel that you are far away or even irrelevant to
my daily life. But when I read your promises in the Bible, I
am reminded that you are anything but distant and aloof.
You promise to be with me in the form of the Holy Spirit.
You promise to forgive my sins, to give me peace of heart
and mind, to carry my burdens, and to give me rest. How
much more meaningful and relevant could your promises
be? With you always by my side, I don't need to be afraid.
With you forgiving my sins, I don't need to feel guilty anymore. I am motivated to overcome temptations instead
of succumbing to them. God, I am so thankful that you
offer to carry my burdens so I can be free from worry and
anxiety. I praise you for the peace of mind and heart these
promises bring! Thank you, God, that you promise all
of these things and that you are faithful in keeping your
promises. Help me to cling to your eternal promises each
day so I will never forget how close and relevant you really
are.

*O LORD, God of Israel, there is no God like you in all of
heaven above or on the earth below. You keep your covenant
and show unfailing love to all who walk before you in
wholehearted devotion.* 1 KINGS 8:23

☼ **A prayer for PEACE**
When I'm looking for peace in a world full of conflict

DEAR JESUS,

So many things rob me of peace—conflict, uncertainty, busyness, worry, fear. How can I have peace amid so much turmoil? Lord, I want to have the quiet, unshakable peace that comes from placing my trust fully in you, the same peace that allowed you to go to the cross on my behalf. Help me to rest in the knowledge that my treasure is truly in heaven.

[Jesus said] "I have told you all this so that you may have peace in me. Here on earth you will have many trials and sorrows. But take heart, because I have overcome the world."
JOHN 16:33

DAY 350 *Prayerful Moment*

☼ **A prayer for GUIDANCE**
When I don't know where to turn for guidance

HEAVENLY FATHER,

When travelers don't know where they are going, they rely on an accurate map. In the same way, I must realize my own spiritual limitations and rely on the truth of your Word. I am on a journey toward my eternal home in heaven. I trust you to lead me and guide me.

Their words are like a lamp shining in a dark place—until the Day dawns, and Christ the Morning Star shines in your hearts. 2 PETER 1:19

DAY 351

☀ **A prayer for GRACE**
When I mourn over the sin in my life

O LORD,

Whenever I sin I lose so much—my intimate relationship with you, a keen knowledge of your plan for me, the Holy Spirit's empowerment to live the Christian life, wholeness within myself and in my relationships, and the ability to be a pure and effective witness. I am filled with grief because I am mourning all that my sin has caused me to lose. May my sorrow lead me to bow at your feet and ask you for forgiveness, for I know you will give it if I ask with a sincere heart. And then may I accept your promise to wipe the slate clean. Lord, may your mercy increase my desire to follow you so that my life can testify to your ability to transform a sinner into one of your saints.

The LORD is close to the brokenhearted; he rescues those whose spirits are crushed. PSALM 34:18

☼ A prayer of **FORGIVENESS**
When I need to forgive someone

DEAR JESUS,

Your example demonstrates that forgiveness is the pathway to freedom in relationships. But like salvation, forgiveness is both a decision and a process. Someone has hurt me, and while I've decided to forgive him, it will be a long time before we freely trust one another. Jesus, you're teaching me that sometimes I must decide to forgive even before I have feelings of mercy. It's a decision based on your command to forgive others. While it's difficult, I know that when I forgive someone who has wronged me, I am freed from bitterness and resentment. Lord Jesus, I need help to release the hurt inflicted on me. I want to let it go so I will be healed and free to grow beyond the pain. When I think of all that you have forgiven me and the freedom it has brought me, with your help I can certainly forgive this person who has hurt me.

If you forgive those who sin against you, your heavenly Father will forgive you. MATTHEW 6:14

☼ A prayer about GENEROSITY
When I'd like to be more generous with what I have

DEAR GOD,

What I spend my money on reveals what I care about most. Lord, what do my spending habits say about me? Probably that I tend to be focused on myself instead of others. How can I be a more generous and cheerful giver? I know that what's significant is not what I have but what I do with what I have, for you look at the heart. O God, is my heart where you want it to be? Please reveal to me the true nature of my heart. Help me see myself as I really am so I can know what I need to change to have a generous heart more like yours. Please teach me the discipline of generosity, and may this discipline of giving transform my heart. Generosity is the opposite of selfishness, and selfishness is a cousin of pride, greed, stinginess, and hard-heartedness—all traits that destroy relationships. But generosity promotes giving, trust, mercy, and putting others' needs above my own—all traits that build relationships. May you grow those characteristics in me. And as I more fully realize that everything I have is a gift from you, my generous God, may I be motivated to share my material resources more freely.

You must each decide in your heart how much to give. And don't give reluctantly or in response to pressure. "For God loves a person who gives cheerfully." 2 CORINTHIANS 9:7

⚙ **A prayer for JOY**
When I seek lasting joy despite life's ups and downs

DEAR GOD,

You created me to have feelings, so I shouldn't be surprised when I experience emotional or spiritual highs and lows. However, I know that lasting joy and contentment run much deeper than momentary emotions. Lasting joy is like a strong current that runs deep beneath the stormy surface of my feelings. It is sharing with others the blessings of your presence. Joy is the sense of security that comes only from being held by you, an almighty God. It is the peace of knowing that you accept me and want me to be with you forever in eternity. It is the quiet confidence I experience when I let you guide me at all times and in all things, knowing that wherever you guide me is in my best interests. No emotional ups and downs can shake that kind of strong foundation. I praise you because in you I have found the source of true and lasting joy.

Let the godly rejoice. Let them be glad in God's presence. Let them be filled with joy. PSALM 68:3

☼ **A prayer about the HOLY SPIRIT**
When I need confirmation of the Holy Spirit's power

O HOLY SPIRIT,

You are God, living in perfect union with the Father and the Son. What a glorious mystery this is. You live in the heart of everyone who calls upon the name of Jesus. When I give you control of my life, you release your power within me—power to resist temptation, to serve and love you and others, to endure when I am at the end of my rope, to have wisdom in all circumstances, and to persevere in godly living here on earth with the promise of eternal life in heaven. Thank you for providing the energy, the wisdom, and the resources I need to do whatever you ask me to do.

Let the Holy Spirit guide your lives. Then you won't be doing what your sinful nature craves. The sinful nature wants to do evil, which is just the opposite of what the Spirit wants. And the Spirit gives us desires that are the opposite of what the sinful nature desires. GALATIANS 5:16-17

✺ **A prayer about the POWER OF GOD**
When I'm feeling powerless

ALMIGHTY GOD,

Thank you that you've chosen to reveal your power through weak and imperfect people. When I am weak, it is only by your strength that I am able to accomplish what I could not do on my own. I'm grateful to have your Holy Spirit and your power working through me. Thank you!

Each time he said, "My grace is all you need. My power works best in weakness." So now I am glad to boast about my weaknesses, so that the power of Christ can work through me.
2 CORINTHIANS 12:9

DAY 357 *Prayerful Moment*

✺ **A prayer about being TIRED**
When I'm exhausted but have to keep going

DEAR JESUS,

I long to rest, but this is one of those times in life when I cannot take a break. Though it is nearly impossible to get enough rest right now, I know my weariness is an opportunity to experience your faithfulness. Please empower me by your Spirit to finish the task as strongly as I began. Let my weariness be the vehicle by which your strength and power shine brightly. I pray that, though my body is weary, you will bring me peace as I press on.

Be strong in the Lord and in his mighty power.
EPHESIANS 6:10

☼ A prayer about WORTH
When I struggle with my sense of self-worth

O LORD,

I come before you feeling not so good about myself. Where do I get my sense of self-worth? Do I need to look attractive to feel good about myself? Do I need a big accomplishment that everyone notices? Do I need a job that impresses my friends? Do I need a lot of things to add value to my life? This is a precarious way to live, but I am afraid I am doing exactly this—equating my worth with something I have or something I've done. It causes me always to be scrambling after more just to feel good about myself. The worst part is that it keeps my eyes off you, O Lord, the only one who can give my life a real sense of worth. I am amazed at how much you value me! You created me and knew me intimately before I was even born. And you loved me so much, you rescued me from eternal punishment for my sins through Jesus' death and resurrection. No matter what I do or possess, it pales in comparison to the value of my relationship with you, Lord. Thank you for your love, forgiveness, and grace to me. You are worthy of my praise, gratitude, and love in return.

How precious are your thoughts about me, O God.
PSALM 139:17

☼ **A prayer for PEACE**

With all the upheaval in my life, how can I maintain a sense of peace?

O GOD,

I could use a little more peace. It seems that the one thing that never changes is change! Just as I think life has settled down a bit, another life-altering change rises up to test me. I guess part of life is learning to expect these new challenges. I need to stop being so upset when my plans are thwarted. Instead, please instill in me the commitment to build my life on the changeless principles and promises that you give in your Word. When I experience upheaval, may I turn to your Word to maintain my perspective and stay grounded. Peace in my life may have to wait until heaven, but I can have peace in my heart right now—and that doesn't have to change when new challenges come along. O God, I want to make it a priority to approach life with this eternal perspective. May I rest in the security of knowing that my future is in your hands.

You will keep in perfect peace all who trust in you, all whose thoughts are fixed on you! ISAIAH 26:3

⚙ **A prayer about GIVING**
*When I want to give to others based on how much
God has given me*

LORD,

Giving is such a remarkable concept that it could only have
originated in the heart of a generous God like you. You
pour out more blessings on me than I could ever deserve.
The gift of life, the gift of love, the gift of salvation, the
gift of eternity in heaven—all of these are priceless. My
possessions are generally a tangible result of what I have
invested through time, energy, and talent. But who I am,
my very character, is always a direct result of what I have
invested of myself with you and others. One of the great
promises of the Bible is that the more I give, the more
I receive—not necessarily in material possessions, but in
spiritual and eternal rewards. Whatever I receive in this
life, whether material or spiritual, is because you have
given it to me. Nothing I receive is of my own doing, so
everything I receive I can pass along to bless others.

*Everything we have has come from you, and we give you
only what you first gave us!* I CHRONICLES 29:14

☀ **A prayer about FAITHFULNESS**
When I tell of God's faithfulness to the next
generation

LORD GOD,

Today, I ask for the courage to reveal your faithfulness to the next generation—something that's both a privilege and an obligation. I see your faithfulness everywhere around me, and I want to leave a rich spiritual heritage by building this awareness into the minds of my children and grandchildren. Let my words and actions "sing a duet" of faithfulness to you so I can give my children an example to treasure throughout their lifetimes. This has far more lasting value than any other kind of inheritance I might leave behind. Hear my prayer, Lord, for I long for others to rest in your unfailing love and faithfulness.

The love of the LORD remains forever with those who fear him. His salvation extends to the children's children of those who are faithful to his covenant, of those who obey his commandments! PSALM 103:17-18

☀ **A prayer about LOVE**
When I need to see love in perspective

O LORD JESUS,

If I get anything right in this life, help me to get love right. I want to love you and others with the unconditional love you model for me. Too often I think of love as just a feeling. I know that's part of it, but according to your Word, it's so much more than that. You show me that it is a commitment. Jesus, please help me to remember that love is not dependent on warm feelings alone but on a consistent and courageous decision to extend myself for the well-being of someone else. You perfectly demonstrated your unconditional love when you made the loving commitment to lay down your life to save me and all people from our sins. When I love you with all my heart, soul, and strength, I am making a commitment to develop a relationship with you, the Creator of the universe. Thank you that you loved me first and daily pursue me with your love.

The LORD says, "I will rescue those who love me. I will protect those who trust in my name. When they call on me, I will answer; I will be with them in trouble. I will rescue and honor them. I will reward them with a long life and give them my salvation." PSALM 91:14-16

☼ A prayer of CELEBRATION
When I have many reasons to praise God

LORD GOD,

You have given me much to celebrate, and I praise you with great joy! As I enjoy your blessings, my hope in you grows. Thank you for your timely provision and abundant kindness. I look forward to the even greater joys I will experience someday in heaven. In the meantime, I honor you and worship you by celebrating all you have done.

Let all who take refuge in you rejoice; let them sing joyful praises forever. Spread your protection over them, that all who love your name may be filled with joy. PSALM 5:11

DAY 364 *Prayerful Moment*

☼ A prayer of REMEMBRANCE
When I remember what God has done for me

LORD,

Today I pause to reflect on where I've been, where I am now, and where I am going. I'm so thankful for all you have done in my life. May I never forget your work of love and mercy. Today, Lord, I will speak of your faithfulness. And may I build a legacy of faith for future generations.

I will teach you hidden lessons from our past—stories we have heard and known, stories our ancestors handed down to us. We will not hide these truths from our children; we will tell the next generation about the glorious deeds of the LORD, about his power and his mighty wonders. PSALM 78:1-4

☀ **A prayer about FINISHING WELL**
When I need strength to finish well

O LORD,

I want to finish well. As the years march on, it is painful to realize I no longer possess the physical skills or energy I used to have. But even more frightening are the persistent temptations that threaten to wear me down. The enemy knows my weaknesses, and day after day, month after month, year after year, he knows which temptations are most likely to attract me. I am afraid that, in a moment of weakness, I will sin boldly and then have to live with the tragic consequences. Please keep me away from circumstances where the temptation will be too strong for me to overcome. I don't want to let an evening of fun ruin a lifetime of faithfulness. Lord, may I finish strong in my walk of faith. When I am old and gray and depart this earth, I will meet you face-to-face. I pray that you will be able to say, "Well done, my good and faithful servant."

I am certain that God, who began the good work within you, will continue his work until it is finally finished on the day when Christ Jesus returns. PHILIPPIANS 1:6

TOPICAL INDEX

Abilities | Days 9, 243
Absence | Day 89
Absolute Truth | Day 20
Acceptance | Days 153, 194
Accomplishments | Days 11, 222
Accountability | Days 61, 248
Adaptability | Day 209
Addiction | Day 198
Admiration | Day 300
Adversity | Days 53, 240
Advice | Days 68, 343
Affirmation | Days 47, 315
Anger | Day 81
Anticipation | Days 3, 108
Apathy | Day 39
Apology | Days 66, 305
Appreciation | Day 328
Armor of God | Day 268
Assertiveness | Day 299
Assurance | Day 201
Attitude | Day 130
Authenticity | Day 280
Availability | Day 34
Backsliding | Day 218
Beauty | Days 97, 339
Beginnings | Day 17
Belonging | Day 26
Betrayal | Day 283
Blessings | Days 84, 325
Brokenness | Days 308, 331
Busyness | Days 147, 272
Call of God | Days 8, 67, 275
Care | Day 80
Celebration | Days 105, 363
Challenges | Days 4, 336
Change | Days 123, 251, 327
Children | Days 92, 340
Choices | Days 71, 255
Church | Days 111, 154, 293, 326
Circumstances | Days 69, 110, 230
Comfort | Days 121, 319

Commitment | Days 41, 64, 125
Communication | Day 292
Comparison | Day 285
Compassion | Day 168
Compatibility | Day 83
Competition | Day 133
Complacency | Day 264
Compliments | Day 244
Compromise | Day 281
Confession | Days 6, 274
Confidence | Day 276
Conflict | Day 232
Conformity | Day 173
Conscience | Days 177, 180
Consequences | Day 182
Conversation | Day 236
Conviction | Day 183
Courage | Days 187, 196
Creativity | Days 162, 235
Crisis | Days 229, 254, 257
Criticism | Days 159, 239
Danger | Day 242
Death | Day 260
Decisions | Day 241
Deliverance | Day 199
Demands | Day 186
Dependence | Days 51, 265
Depression | Days 54, 150, 217
Desirability | Day 46
Desires | Days 158, 224, 256
Differences | Days 77, 270, 284
Dignity | Day 163
Disappointment | Day 320
Disapproval | Day 72
Discernment | Day 101
Discipline | Days 213, 310
Discontentment | Day 298
Discouragement | Days 62, 269, 322
Distractions | Day 297
Doubt | Days 63, 197, 234, 304

Emotion | Day 206
Empathy | Day 204
Emptiness | Day 207
Encouragement | Days 104, 184, 227
Endurance | Days 219, 303
Enemies | Days 119, 288
Energy | Days 90, 321
Eternal Life | Day 228
Eternity | Day 112
Evil | Day 185
Example | Day 312
Excellence | Day 192
Expectations | Day 102
Experience | Day 36
Faith | Days 82, 126
Faithfulness | Days 335, 361
Family | Day 342
Fear | Day 210
Fearing God | Day 306
Fellowship | Day 137
Finishing Well | Day 365
Flexibility | Day 156
Forgiveness | Days 155, 216, 352
Freedom | Day 164
Friendship with God | Day 103
Fun | Day 202
Future | Days 106, 267
Generosity | Day 353
Gentleness | Day 160
Giving | Day 360
Goals | Day 7
God's Hand | Day 33
God's Timing | Day 87
God's Will | Day 277
Gossip | Day 37
Grace | Days 152, 332, 351
Grief | Day 263
Growth | Day 1
Guidance | Days 289, 350
Guilt | Day 220
Habits | Day 24
Happiness | Day 94
Hard-Heartedness | Day 50

Healing | Day 75
Heart | Days 76, 203
Help | Day 131
Holiness | Day 165
Holy Spirit | Days 27, 91, 215, 355
Honesty | Day 191
Hope | Days 5, 258
Hospitality | Day 140
Humility | Days 116, 317
Hurts | Day 161
Imagination | Days 190, 296
Impact | Day 245
Impossible | Day 318
Influence | Day 290
Initiative | Days 2, 78
Injustice | Day 337
Insecurity | Day 261
Inspiration | Day 114
Integrity | Days 95, 238
Involvement | Day 246
Irritation | Day 252
Joy | Days 149, 354
Knowledge | Day 279
Leadership | Day 113
Letting Go | Days 79, 88
Limitations | Day 313
Listening | Days 73, 237, 259
Loneliness | Day 338
Loss | Day 266
Love | Days 48, 174, 291, 362
Loyalty | Day 55
Meaning | Day 195
Meditation | Day 14
Memories | Day 86
Mentoring | Day 129
Mercy | Day 23
Miracles | Day 295
Mistakes | Day 181
Mystery | Days 107, 346
Needs | Day 166
Neglect | Day 233
Neighbors | Day 341
Obedience | Days 141, 144

Opportunities | Day 70
Opposition | Day 178
Overwhelmed | Day 99
Pain | Days 142, 316
Passion | Day 100
Past | Day 311
Patience | Days 21, 211
Peace | Days 309, 349, 359
Perfection | Day 42
Persecution | Day 208
Perseverance | Day 347
Pleasure | Day 314
Potential | Days 22, 65
Power of God | Days 74, 214, 356
Praise | Day 169
Prayer | Days 200, 271
Preparation | Day 179
Presence of God | Days 13, 302
Pretending | Day 139
Priorities | Day 307
Promises of God | Days 35, 250, 348
Provision | Day 329
Purpose | Days 127, 247, 334
Pursued by God | Day 273
Quiet Times | Day 18
Quitting | Day 189
Reconciliation | Day 212
Regrets | Day 32
Relationship | Days 31, 253
Relevance | Day 262
Remembrance | Day 364
Renewal | Day 151
Repentance | Day 122
Reputation | Day 40
Respect | Day 124
Responsibility | Day 145
Rest | Day 157
Rewards | Day 171
Risk | Days 52, 287
Romance | Day 49
Seeking God | Day 57
Self-Denial | Day 249
Self-Esteem | Day 58
Service | Days 128, 344

Sharing | Day 345
Significance | Day 115
Simplicity | Day 136
Sin | Day 29
Sorrow | Days 118, 170
Sovereignty of God | Day 45
Spiritual Dryness | Days 19, 294
Spiritual Gifts | Day 85
Spiritual Growth | Day 231
Spiritual Warfare | Day 132
Stewardship | Day 135
Strength | Days 175, 223, 333
Stress | Day 188
Stubbornness | Day 134
Success | Days 138, 286
Supernatural | Day 167
Surprise | Day 205
Surrender | Days 59, 98
Temptation | Days 28, 172, 301
Tenderness | Day 323
Testing | Day 225
Thankfulness | Day 330
Thoughts | Days 93, 226
Time | Day 44
Tired | Days 146, 357
Tithing | Day 10
Transformation | Day 12
Trust | Day 25
Truth | Day 96
Unity | Day 117
Value | Day 143
Values | Day 43
Victory | Day 148
Vision | Day 15
Vulnerability | Day 60
Waiting | Day 56
Warnings | Day 324
Wisdom | Days 120, 282
Witnessing | Day 176
Words | Day 38
Work | Days 16, 193
Worry | Day 221
Worship | Days 109, 278
Worth | Days 30, 358